The New Orleans Saints: History, Hurricane Katrina, Drew Brees, Super Bowl XLIV and Seasons 2006 - 2010

Jenny Reese

Contents

Articles

History of the Saints

The Field

Hurrican Katrina

Seasons 2006-2010

Super Bowl XLIV

Drew Brees

Players and Head Coaches

Retired Numbers

References

New Orleans Saints

The **New Orleans Saints** are a professional American football team based in New Orleans, Louisiana. They are the current champions of the National Football League (NFL) and play in the South Division of the National Football Conference (NFC).

The Saints were founded on November 1, 1966 as an expansion team and played their home games at Tulane Stadium through the 1974 season. They went more than a decade before they managed to finish a season with a .500 record, two decades before having a winning season, and over four decades before reaching the Super Bowl. The team's first successful years were from 1987–1992, when the team made the playoffs four times and had winning records in the non-playoff seasons. In the 2000 season, the Saints defeated the then-defending Super Bowl champion St. Louis Rams for the team's first playoff win.

The Saints reached the NFC Championship Game in the 2006 season but lost 39–14 to the Chicago Bears. They repeated this feat in their most successful season in 2009, this time winning the game and their first conference championship to send them to their first Super Bowl appearance. At Super Bowl XLIV, the Saints won the city of New Orleans its first league championship, beating the Indianapolis Colts 31-17.

Since 1975, the Saints' home stadium has been the Louisiana Superdome, except for the 2005 disruption caused by Hurricane Katrina.

History

Early history

First the brainchild of local sports entrepreneur Dave Dixon, who also founded the Louisiana Superdome and the USFL, the Saints were actually secretly born in a backroom deal brought about by Congressman Hale Boggs, Senator Russell Long and NFL Commissioner Pete Rozelle. The NFL needed congressional approval of the proposed AFL-NFL merger. Dixon and a local civic group had been seeking a NFL franchise for over 5 years, and had hosted record crowds to NFL exhibition games. To seal the merger, Rozelle arrived in New Orleans within a week, and announced on November 1, 1966 that the NFL officially had awarded the city of New Orleans an NFL franchise. Named for the great jazz song most identified with New Orleans – "When the Saints Go Marching In", the franchise was announced in a great coincidence on November 1, which is the Catholic All Saints' Day. Boggs' Congressional committee in turn quickly approved the NFL merger. John W. Mecom, Jr., a young oilman from Houston, became the team's first majority stockholder. The team's colors, black and gold, symbolized both Mecom's and New Orleans' strong ties to the oil ("black gold") industry. Trumpeter Al Hirt was part owner of the team, and his rendition of "When the Saints Go Marching In" was made the official fight song.

That first season started with a 94 yard opening kickoff return for a touchdown by John Gilliam, but the Saints lost that game 27–13 to the Los Angeles Rams at Tulane Stadium. Their first season record was 3–11, which set an NFL record for most wins by an expansion team. However, they could not manage to finish as high as second in their division until 1979. That 1979 team and the 1983 team were the only ones to even finish at .500 until 1987.

One of the franchise's shining moments came on November 8, 1970, when Tom Dempsey kicked an NFL record-breaking 63-yard field goal to defeat the Detroit Lions by a score of 19–17 in the final seconds of the game. This record, although equaled 29 years later by Jason Elam of the Denver Broncos, has yet to be broken.

In 1980, the Saints lost their first 14 games, prompting local sportscaster Bernard "Buddy D" Diliberto to advise Saints supporters to wear paper bags over their heads at the team's home games; many bags rendered the club's name as the "'Aints" rather than the "Saints." The practice of wearing a bag over one's head then spread rapidly, first to fans of other poorly performing teams within the NFL, and ultimately to those of other American team sports, and has become a firmly established custom throughout the United States.

The Jim Mora Era

Current Saints owner Tom Benson acquired the franchise in 1985, and hired Jim Finks as general manager and Jim Mora as head coach. That combination provided the Saints with their first-ever winning record and playoff appearance, going 12–3 in 1987, which had one fewer game than normal due to a players' strike. Another playoff berth would follow in 1990, and the club's first division title came in 1991. During Mora's tenure the Saints made the playoffs four times, with teams marked by strong defenses led by the "Dome Patrol" linebacking corps, but they were never able to win a playoff game. Mora coached the Saints until the middle of the 1996 season, when he stepped down halfway through a 3–13 season.

The Mike Ditka Era

After the end of the 1996 season, ironically as Diliberto had suggested before Mora's resignation, former Chicago Bears coach Mike Ditka was hired to replace Mora. Although this initially generated a lot of excitement among Saints fans, Ditka's tenure ended up being a failure. The Saints went 6–10 in their first two seasons under Ditka (1997 and 1998). During the 1999 NFL Draft, Ditka traded all of his picks for that season, as well as the first-round and third-round picks for the following season, to the Washington Redskins in order to draft University of Texas Heisman Trophy running back Ricky Williams in the first round. Ditka and Williams had a mock wedding picture taken to commemorate the occasion. However, Ditka, most of his coaching staff, and general manager Bill Kuharich were fired at the end of the 1999 season due to the club's 3–13 record.

The Jim Haslett Era

Jim Haslett held the post from 2000 to 2005. In his first year, he took the team to the playoffs but lost to the Minnesota Vikings a week after beating the St. Louis Rams for the team's first ever playoff win. After winning the 2000 NFL Executive of the Year Award, General Manager Randy Mueller was fired between the 2001 and 2002 seasons without explanation by Benson. The Saints failed to make the playoffs in 2001 and 2002, although in the latter year they had the distinction of beating the eventual Super Bowl XXXVII champion Tampa Bay Buccaneers in both of their regular season meetings, only the second team to do so in NFL history.

In 2003, the Saints again missed the playoffs after finishing 8–8. The 2004 season started poorly for the Saints, as they went 2–4 through their first six games and 4–8 through their first twelve games. At that point Haslett's job appeared to be in jeopardy; however, he managed to win the three straight games leading up to the season finale, leaving the Saints in playoff contention in the final week of the season. In week 17, the Saints defeated division rivals Carolina; however, the Saints needed other results to break their way and when the St. Louis Rams beat the New York Jets the Saints were eliminated despite having beaten the Rams, who finished with the same record. The Rams, Saints, and Vikings all were 8–8, with the Rams having a 7–5 conference record, Saints 6–6, and the Vikings 5–7. The Rams received the #1 wild-card due to having the best conference record out of the 3, followed by the Vikings due to the 33–16 loss handed to the Saints in Week 3. Haslett was fired after the 2005 season, in which the Saints finished 3–13 and did not play one regular season contest in New Orleans due to Hurricane Katrina. On January 17, 2006, the Saints hired Sean Payton as their new head coach.

Effect of Hurricane Katrina

Due to the damage Hurricane Katrina caused to the Superdome and the New Orleans area, the Saints' scheduled 2005 home opener against the New York Giants was moved to Giants Stadium. The remainder of their 2005 home games were split between the Alamodome in San Antonio, Texas, and LSU's Tiger Stadium in Baton Rouge, Louisiana.

The Sean Payton & Drew Brees Era

2006

On March 23, the Saints announced that the team's two 2006 preseason games were to be played at Shreveport, Louisiana and Jackson, Mississippi.After a $185 million renovation of the historic stadium, on April 6 the Saints released their 2006 schedule, with all home games scheduled to be played at the Superdome. On September 19, Saints owner Tom Benson announced that the team had sold out the Louisiana Superdome for the entire season with season tickets alone (70,001 seats), a first in franchise history.

The September 25, 2006 home opener, the first home game in New Orleans after Hurricane Katrina, was won by the Saints 23–3 against the Atlanta Falcons, who were undefeated in the 2006 season at that time. The attendance for the game was a sellout crowd of 70,003. Meanwhile, the broadcast of the game was ESPN's highest-ever rated program to date, with an 11.8 rating, and viewership by 10,850,000 homes. It was the most-watched program for the night, broadcast or cable, and was the second-highest rated cable program of all time at the time. Green Day and U2 performed "Wake Me Up When September Ends" and "The Saints Are Coming" , respectively, before the game. The game received a 2007 ESPY award for "Best Moment in Sports".

On December 17, 2006, the Saints clinched their third division title and their first NFC South title in franchise history. For the first time in Saints' history, they clinched their NFC South title on their home field. Sean Payton became the second consecutive Saints coach to win a division title in his first season. After a loss by the Dallas Cowboys to the Philadelphia Eagles on Christmas Day 2006, the Saints clinched a first-round playoff bye for the first time in franchise history.

After the first-round bye, the Saints beat the Philadelphia Eagles 27–24 in the Superdome in the 2006 Divisional Playoffs. No team had ever had such a poor record in the prior year (3–13) and then gone on to a league or conference championship game since the 1999 St. Louis Rams who advanced to win their first Super Bowl after being 4–12 the season before. Since the Saints' only previous playoff win was in the wild card round, this was the farthest the Saints had ever advanced at the time. The victory was only the second playoff win in team history. The season ended on January 21, 2007 when the Saints lost 39–14 to the Chicago Bears in the NFC Championship game.

2007

The Saints announced that for the second year in a row, the Louisiana Superdome had sold out every ticket for the season. Additionally, all luxury boxes had been sold out for the season. Both of these statistics are particularly surprising given that the city-proper has about 300,000 people or 150,000 fewer people than July 2005 population data (though the metro area still accounts for 1.2 million people)..

The first game of the season was against the defending Super Bowl XLI champion Indianapolis Colts. The Saints lost this game, 41–10, and lost their next three games. In one of these three games, against the Tennessee Titans, the Saints lost running back Deuce McAllister for the season with his second career (second time in three seasons) ACL tear. After winning their first game, against the Seattle Seahawks, two weeks later, the team went on a four-game winning streak to bring their record to an even 4–4. After reaching 7–7, the Saints lost their final two games to finish 7–9.

2008

Following a disappointing 7-9 record in the 2007 season, the Saints ended the 2008 season 8-8. Failing to qualify for the post season for the second straight year, the Saints found themselves struggling on offense and defense. The Saints would match the explosive offense they had in the 2006 season but the defense was a disappointment. Drew Brees ended the 2008 season just 15 yards short of tying Dan Marino single season of 5084 total passing yards. Lance Moore was 72 yards short of his first 1000 yard season.

2009

The 2009 season was the team's most successful season, which culminated in the franchise's first league championship win against the Indianapolis Colts in Super Bowl XLIV. After achieving a record of 13–0 with their win over the Atlanta Falcons, it marked the Saints' best start to a season in its franchise history. The result clinched an NFC playoff berth, a bye in the first round of the playoffs. By winning their first 13 games, the Saints also set the record for the longest undefeated season opening (13–0) by an NFC team since the AFL–NFL merger, eclipsing the previous record (12–0) held by the 1985 Chicago Bears. However, they would fall victim to the Dallas Cowboys in week 15, going on to end the season with a 3 game losing streak.

Although its opponents would include winners of 9 of the last 15 NFL MVP awards, the team advanced to the 2009 NFC Championship game where they defeated the Minnesota Vikings 31–28 in overtime to win their first Super Bowl appearance in franchise history. Television ratings for Super Bowl 44 were the highest for any TV program, sports or otherwise, in history. Since the win, two media writers have referred to the Saints as "America's Team", as their successful bid to win the Super Bowl was seen by many to represent the city's resurgence after the devastating Hurricane Katrina.

2010

The Saints 2010 season will begin in the Superdome as the Super Bowl Champion New Orleans Saints will be hosting the Minnesota Vikings in a 2009-10 NFC Championship Game rematch. It will be played on Thursday September 9, 2010 on NBC, making it the first time the Saints have opened the NFL's season at home. The Saints successfully resigned all but one of its players that started last season's Super Bowl run. Scott Fujita, a starting outside linebacker (playing the "Sam" or Strongside position), signed with the Cleveland Browns in the offseason and is the only player that was not under contract not to be resigned.

Logos and uniforms

Except for minor modifications, the Saints' logo and uniforms have basically remained the same since the club debuted in 1967. The team's logo is a fleur-de-lis (a symbol of the City of New Orleans and of France's Bourbon monarchy), while its uniform design consists of gold helmets, gold pants, and either black or white jerseys. Minor changes to the uniform stripes and trim have been made throughout the years. The team wore black helmets during the 1969 preseason, but NFL commissioner Pete Rozelle barred the Saints from using the helmets during the regular season, since owner John Mecom, Jr. did not notify the league office of the change.

The Saints predominantly wore white at home when the club played at Tulane Stadium from 1967 through 1974 (except in 1969 and 1970), forcing opponents to wear dark colors in the subtropical climate of New Orleans. When the surface at Tulane Stadium switched from natural grass to AstroTurf in 1971, field temperatures became hotter still. In Archie Manning's first game, in the 1971 season opener against the Los Angeles Rams, temperatures on the field reached as high as . The heavily favored Rams wilted in the stifling heat, and the Saints claimed their first-ever victory over their NFC West rivals, 24–20, on Manning's 1-yard quarterback sneak on the last play of the game.

The Saints switched to white pants in 1975, coinciding with the team's move from Tulane Stadium to the Superdome. One year later, they started to wear black pants with their white jerseys, a move influenced by coach Hank Stram, who introduced red pants to the Kansas City Chiefs' uniforms in 1968. In an October 3, 1976 home game against the Houston Oilers, Hank Stram used the Saints' road uniforms, the white jerseys and black pants. The Saints lost that game 31–26. During the 1981–82 seasons (Bum Phillips' first two seasons as coach), the team wore white jerseys with black pants at home, but reverted back to the black jerseys and white pants for 1983. They reverted back to wearing gold pants with both their black and white jerseys in 1986 under new coach Jim E. Mora. From 1986 through 1995, the sleeves of the jerseys and sides of the pants featured a logo with a fleur-de-lis inside an outline of the state of Louisiana. The logo replaced the striping pattern that had been on the uniforms since the team's inception; save for color variations, the striping pattern was similar to that used by the Washington Redskins (until 1979), Green Bay Packers (until 1997), and Cleveland Browns (still in use), which is likely why the change was made. That logo was removed in 1996 and replaced with a fleur-de-lis on both the sleeves and sides of the pants.

From 1996 through 1998, the Saints returned to gold numbers on both the white and black jerseys, but complaints about the numbers on the white jerseys being too difficult to read forced the numbers on the white jerseys to be changed to black in 1999. The Saints wore black pants with a wide gold stripe with their white jerseys in 1999, but following a 3–13 season and the dismissal of coach Mike Ditka, the black pants were mothballed by new coach Jim Haslett.

2000s

In 2000, the Saints won their first playoff game as they hosted the St. Louis Rams and after having a better road record than home record, they wore their white jerseys, helping them get a 31–28 win over the defending champion Rams. The defining play of the game came with the Saints clinging to a three-point lead with minutes to play. The Saints punted to the Rams' Az-Zahir Hakim (who would play one season for the Saints in 2005), who fumbled the punt deep in Rams' territory. Brian Milne recovered for the Saints, who then ran out the clock to preserve the victory.

In 2001, they wore their white jerseys in the first six home games. During that same year, they primarily wore black pants with both their white and black jerseys. They became the first NFL team to wear all-black uniforms in a week 5 road game against the Carolina Panthers, and again in weeks 16 and 17 in home games against the Washington Redskins and San Francisco 49ers.

In 2002, the Saints wore black pants with their white jerseys (except for the final road game, a 20–13 loss in Cincinnati when they went back to the gold pants), and gold pants with their black jerseys, a gold alternate jersey, and a 1967-style throwback uniform. But one season later, they stopped using the alternates and again reverted back to wearing gold pants with both their black and white jerseys.

The team introduced a gold alternate jersey (worn with the black pants) during a December 15, 2002 game versus the Minnesota Vikings, a 32–31 loss, but have never worn them since then. Because of the metallic gold's bright color, the gold jerseys were considered the "light" jersey in the game, so the Vikings wore their purple home jerseys as the "dark" colored team. One team must wear "dark" and one team must wear "light", this was done because of black & white t.v. broadcasts so viewers could tell the teams apart. the only exception being if both teams are wearing throwback uniforms, such as Thanksgiving Classic games. Today only the New England Patriots have a "light" jersey (their alternate, a bright metallic silver) that isn't white in which the other team would wear their colored, or "dark" jerseys against them since the third jersey rule was implemented in the NFL in 2002.

The Saints also introduced a 1967-style throwback uniform in a 23–20 win in week 13 (December 1) against the Tampa Bay Buccaneers. This also was never worn again but re-introduction of the jerseys in stores suggests they may make a comeback as the Saints' alternate uniform.

In 2006, to honor their return to Louisiana, the Saints wore a patch on their uniforms with an outline of the State of Louisiana with a fleur-de-lis superimposed, similar to the logo from the 1980s.

The Saints originally planned to wear white jerseys at home for the 2006 season, but during the season, the players voted to wear the black jerseys at home after the second home game. Since the team had informed the NFL office that they planned to wear white jerseys at home, each of the Saints' remaining home opponents would have to agree to New Orleans' request. The Atlanta Falcons, Tampa Bay Buccaneers and Cincinnati Bengals did not agree to the switch, forcing the Saints to wear white jerseys for that game.

Starting in week 13 of the 2006 season, the Saints wore white jerseys with black pants and in a Week 16 game in The Meadowlands against the New York Giants (a 30–7 Saints win), the Saints wore the black pants with their road white jerseys. The Saints later stuck with that combo in the NFC Championship in Chicago.

The Saints wore white jerseys for their first four home games of 2008. Three of the four games the white jerseys with black pants combination were worn at home, while the white jerseys with gold pants combination were worn for the first of those four games. The Saints chose to wear the all-black combination for the October 26 game at Wembley Stadium in London vs. the San Diego Chargers, in which New Orleans was the designated home team. They also wore black jerseys with black pants for the rest of their home games at the Superdome following the game at London.

The Saints wore their white jerseys at home for the first three home games of 2009., with the gold pants combination. They have worn the all-black combo the last two home games. For its run through the 2009 playoffs, the team wore the gold pants.

Statistics

Record vs. opponents

(As of the 2009 NFL season. Includes postseason records.)

|- | Tampa Bay Buccaneers || 21|| 15 || 0 || .583 || L 20-17 OT || December 27, 2009 || New Orleans, LA || |- | Kansas City Chiefs || 5 || 4 || 0 || .556 || W 30–20 || November 10, 2008 || Kansas City, MO || |- | Buffalo Bills || 5 || 4 || 0 || .556 || W 27–7 || September 27, 2009 || Orchard Park, NY || |- | Baltimore/Indianapolis Colts || 6 || 5 || 0 || .545 || W 31–17 || February 7, 2010 || Miami Gardens, FL* || 1–0 postseason |- | New York Jets || 6 || 5 || 0 || .545 || W 24–10 || October 4, 2009 || New Orleans, LA || |- | Detroit Lions || 10 || 9 || 1 || .526 || W 45–27 || September 13, 2009 || New Orleans, LA || |- | St. Louis/Phoenix/Arizona Cardinals || 13 || 13 || 0 || .500 || W 45–14 || January 16, 2010 || New Orleans, LA || 1–0 postseason |- | Los Angeles/Oakland Raiders || 5 || 5 || 1 || .500 || W 34–3 || October 12, 2008 || New Orleans, LA || |- | Seattle Seahawks || 5 || 5 || 0 || .500 || W 28–17 || October 14, 2007 || Seattle, WA || |- | Jacksonville Jaguars || 2 || 2 || 0 || .500 || W 41–24 || November 4, 2007 || New Orleans, LA || |- | Houston Texans || 1 || 1 || 0 || .500 || L 23-10 || November 18, 2007 || Houston, TX || |- | Pittsburgh Steelers || 6 || 7 || 0 || .462 || L 38-31 || November 12, 2006 || Pittsburgh, PA || |- | Cincinnati Bengals || 5 || 6 || 0 || .455 || L 31-16 || November 19, 2006 || New Orleans, LA || |- | Atlanta Falcons || 37 || 45 || 0 || .451 || W 26–23 || December 13, 2009 || Atlanta, GA || 0–1 postseason |- | Los Angeles/St. Louis Rams || 31 || 38 || 0 || .449 || W 28–23 || November 15, 2009 || St. Louis, MO || 1–0 postseason |- | New York Giants || 11 || 14 || 0 || .440 || W 48–27 || October 18, 2009 || New Orleans, LA || |- | Carolina Panthers || 13 || 17 || 0 || .433 || L 23-10 || January 3, 2010 || Charlotte, NC || |- | Chicago Bears || 11 || 15 || 0 || .423 || L 27-24 OT || December 11, 2008 || Chicago, IL || 0–2 postseason |- | Philadelphia Eagles || 11 || 16 || 0 || .407 || W 48–22 || September 20, 2009 || Philadelphia, PA || 1–1 postseason |- | Miami Dolphins || 4 || 6 ||

0 ‖ .400 ‖ W 46–34 ‖ October 25, 2009 ‖ Miami Gardens, FL ‖ |- | Houston Oilers/Tennessee Titans ‖ 4 ‖ 7 ‖ 1 ‖ .375 ‖ L 31-14 ‖ September 24, 2007 ‖ New Orleans, LA ‖ |- | Dallas Cowboys ‖ 8 ‖ 15 ‖ 0 ‖ .348 ‖ L 24-17 ‖ December 19, 2009‖ New Orleans, LA ‖ |- | Washington Redskins ‖ 8 ‖ 15 ‖ 0 ‖ .348 ‖ W 33–30 OT‖ December 6, 2009 ‖ Landover, MD ‖ |- | San Francisco 49ers ‖ 23 ‖ 45 ‖ 2 ‖ .343 ‖ W 31–17 ‖ September 28, 2008 ‖ New Orleans, LA ‖ |- | Green Bay Packers ‖ 7 ‖ 14 ‖ 0 ‖ .333 ‖ W 51–29 ‖ November 24, 2008 ‖ New Orleans, LA ‖ |- | New England Patriots ‖ 4 ‖ 8 ‖ 0 ‖ .333 ‖ W 38–17 ‖ November 30, 2009 ‖ New Orleans, LA ‖ |- | San Diego Chargers ‖ 3 ‖ 7 ‖ 0 ‖ .300 ‖ W 37–32 ‖ October 26, 2008 ‖ London, England** ‖ |- | Minnesota Vikings ‖ 8 ‖ 20 ‖ 0 ‖ .285 ‖ W 31–28 OT ‖ January 24, 2010 ‖ New Orleans, LA ‖ 1–2 postseason |- | Cleveland Browns ‖ 4 ‖ 11 ‖ 0 ‖ .267 ‖ W 19–14 ‖ September 10, 2006 ‖ Cleveland, OH ‖ |- | Baltimore Ravens ‖ 1 ‖ 3 ‖ 0 ‖ .250 ‖ L 35-22 ‖ October 29, 2006 ‖ New Orleans, LA ‖ |- | Denver Broncos ‖ 2 ‖ 7 ‖ 0 ‖ .222 ‖ L 34-32 ‖ September 21, 2008 ‖ Denver, CO ‖ |- | Total ‖ 279 ‖ 377 ‖ 5 ‖ .425 ‖ ‖ ‖ ‖ 5–6 .456

* Super Bowl XLIV. The Saints were designated the visiting team for this game.

** The Saints were designated the home team for this game.

Single-game records

- **Passing Yards:** 510 Drew Brees (November 19, 2006 vs Cincinnati Bengals)
- **Passing Yards Per Attempt:** 16.1 Drew Brees (November 30, 2009 vs New England Patriots)
- **Passing Touchdowns:** 6 Billy Kilmer (November 2, 1969 at St. Louis Cardinals) & Drew Brees (September 13, 2009 vs Detroit Lions)
- **Passer Rating:** 158.3 Drew Brees (November 30, 2009 vs New England Patriots)
- **Consecutive Pass Completions:** 19 Drew Brees (December 27, 2009 vs. Tampa Bay Buccaneers)
- **Rushing Yards:** 206 George Rogers (September 4, 1983 vs St. Louis Cardinals)
- **Rushing Touchdowns:** 3 Reggie Bush (December 3, 2006 vs San Francisco 49ers)
- **Receiving Catches:** 14 Tony Galbreath (September 10, 1978 at Green Bay Packers)
- **Receiving Yards:** 205 Wes Chandler (September 2, 1979 vs Atlanta Falcons)
- **Receiving Touchdowns:** 4 Joe Horn (December 14, 2003 vs New York Giants)
- **Punt Return Yards:** 176 Reggie Bush (October 6, 2008 vs Minnesota Vikings)
- **Pass Interceptions, Game:** 3 Sammy Knight (September 9, 2001 at Buffalo Bills)
- **Longest Interception Return for Touchdown:** 99 yards Darren Sharper (October 4, 2009 vs New York Jets)
- **Field Goals, Game:** 6 Tom Dempsey (November 16, 1969 at New York Giants)
- **Total Touchdowns, Game:** 4 Joe Horn (December 14, 2003 vs New York Giants) & Reggie Bush (December 3, 2006 vs San Francisco 49ers)
- **Points Scored**: 51 at St. Louis Cardinals (November 2, 1969), at Seattle Seahawks (November 21, 1976) & vs Green Bay Packers (November 24, 2008)
- **Margin Of Victory:** 42–0, November 20, 1988 vs Denver Broncos

Single-season records

- **Passing Attempts**: 652 Drew Brees (2007)
- **Passing Completions**: 440 Drew Brees (2007) – NFL Record
- **Passing Completion Percentage**: 70.6 Drew Brees (2009) – NFL Record
- **Passing Yards**: 5,069 Drew Brees (2008) – only the 2nd QB in NFL history to have 5000+ passing yards in a season
- **Passing Touchdowns**: 34 Drew Brees (2008 & 2009)
- **Passing Interceptions**: 22 Aaron Brooks (2001)
- **Passing Rating**: 109.6 Drew Brees (2009)
- **Rushing Attempts**: 378 George Rogers (1981)
- **Rushing Yards**: 1,674 George Rogers (1981)
- **Rushing Touchdowns**: 13 George Rogers (1981), Dalton Hilliard (1989), and Deuce McAllister (2002)
- **Receiving Catches**: 98 Marques Colston (2007)
- **Receiving Yards**: 1,399 Joe Horn (2004)
- **Receiving Touchdowns**: 11 Joe Horn (2004), Marques Colston (2007)
- **Quarterback Sacks**: 17 Pat Swilling (1991) and La'Roi Glover (2000)
- **Pass Interceptions**: 10 Dave Whitsell (1967)
- **Pass Interception Return Yards**: 376 Darren Sharper (2009) – NFL Record
- **Pass Interceptions Returned for Touchdowns**: 3 Darren Sharper (2009)
- **Field Goals Made**: 31 Morten Andersen (1985) and John Carney (2002)
- **Points**: 130 John Carney (2002)
- **Total Touchdowns**: 18 Dalton Hilliard (1989)
- **Punt Return Yards**: 625 Michael Lewis (2002)
- **Kickoff Return Yards**: 1,807 Michael Lewis (2002)
- **Longest Punt**: 81 Tom McNeill (1969)
- **Points Scored, Season**: 510 (2009)
- **Fewest Points Allowed**: 202 (1992)
- **Offensive Yards Gained**: 6,571 (2008)
- **Fewest Quarterback Sacks Allowed**: 13 (2008)

Saints career records

- **Passing Attempts**: 3,335 Archie Manning (1971–75, 77–82), 2,771 Aaron Brooks (2000–05), 2,355 Drew Brees (2006–09)
- **Passing Completions**: 1,849 Archie Manning (1971–75, 77–82), 1,572 Drew Brees (2006–09), 1,565 Aaron Brooks (2000–05)
- **Passing Yards**: 21,734 Archie Manning (1971–75, 77–82), 19,156 Aaron Brooks (2000–05), 18,298 Drew Brees (2006–09)
- **Passing Touchdowns**: 122 Drew Brees (2006–09), 120 Aaron Brooks (2000–2005), 115 Archie Manning (1971–75, 77–82)
- **Passing Interceptions**: 156 Archie Manning (1971–1982), 84 Aaron Brooks (2000–05)
- **Rushing Attempts**: 1,298 Deuce McAllister (2001–2008)
- **Rushing Yards**: 6,096 Deuce McAllister (2001–2008), 4,267 George Rogers (1981–84), 4,164 Dalton Hilliard (1986–93)
- **Rushing Touchdowns**: 49 Deuce McAllister (2001–2008), 39 Dalton Hilliard (1986–93), 28 Chuck Muncie (1976–80)
- **Receiving Catches**: 532 Eric Martin (1985–1993), 523 Joe Horn (2000–06), 309 Danny Abramowicz (1967–73)
- **Receiving Yards**: 7,844 Eric Martin (1985–1993), 7,622 Joe Horn (2000–06), 4,875 Danny Abramowicz (1967–73)
- **Receiving Touchdowns**: 50 Joe Horn (2000–2006), 49 Eric Martin (1985–93), 37 Danny Abramowicz (1967–73)
- **Quarterback Sacks**: 123 Rickey Jackson (1981–1993), 82.5 Wayne Martin (1989–99), 76.5 Pat Swilling (1986–92)
- **Pass Interceptions**: 37 Dave Waymer (1980–1989), 36 Tommy Myers (1972–81), 28 Sammy Knight (1997–2002)
- **Field Goals Made**: 302 Morten Andersen (1982–1994), 140 John Carney (2001–06), 123 Doug Brien (1995–2000)
- **Extra Points Made**: 412 Morten Andersen (1982–1994)
- **Points**: 1,318 Morten Andersen (1982–1994), 631 John Carney (2001–06), 514 Doug Brien (1995–2000)
- **Total Touchdowns**: 55 Deuce McAllister (2001–2008), 53 Dalton Hilliard (1986–1993), 50 Joe Horn (2000–06)
- **Punt Return Yards**: 1,482 Michael Lewis (2001–06), 1,060 Tyrone Hughes (1993–96), 887 Jeff Groth (1981–85)
- **Kickoff Return Yards**: 5,903 Michael Lewis (2001–06), 5,717 Tyrone Hughes (1993–96), 2,836 Rich Mauti (1977–80, 82–83)
- **Games**: 196 Morten Andersen (1982–1994)

Pro Bowl Players

The following Saints players have been named to the Pro bowl:

- **QB** Drew Brees, Archie Manning
- **FB** Tony Baker
- **RB** Deuce McAllister, Dalton Hilliard, Rueben Mayes, George Rogers, Chuck Muncie, Andy Livingston
- **LT** Jamal Brown, William Roaf
- **LG** Brad Edelman, Jake Kupp
- **C** LeCharles Bentley, Joel Hilgenberg, Jonathan Goodwin
- **RG** Jahri Evans
- **RT** Jon Stinchcomb
- **TE** Hoby Brenner, Henry Childs
- **WR** Joe Horn, Eric Martin, Wes Chandler
- **DE** Will Smith, Joe Johnson, Wayne Martin, Renaldo Turnbull, Bruce Clark
- **DT** La'Roi Glover
- **LB** Jonathan Vilma, Mark Fields, Keith Mitchell, Sam Mills, Vaughn Johnson, Pat Swilling, Rickey Jackson
- **CB** Tyrone Hughes, Bennie Thompson, Dave Waymer, Dave Whitsell
- **SS** Roman Harper, Tom Meyers
- **FS** Darren Sharper
- **K** Morten Anderson, Tom Dempsey
- **P** Mitch Berger, Brian Hansen

Super Bowl MVPs

The following Saints players have been named Super Bowl MVP:

- Super Bowl XLIV - Drew Brees

Players of note

Pro Football Hall of Famers

- Doug Atkins DE 1967–1969
- Earl Campbell RB 1984–1985
- Jim Finks GM 1986–1993
- Hank Stram Coach 1976–1977
- Jim Taylor FB 1967

- Mike Ditka Coach 1997–1999 (inducted for playing career with Chicago Bears and other teams, 1961–72)
- Tom Fears Coach 1967–1970 (inducted for playing career, 1948–1956)
- Rickey Jackson LB 1981–1993

Until the selection of Rickey Jackson in 2010, there had been no players in the Hall of Fame whose time with the Saints contributed to their selection; the others were chosen for their work with previous teams. However, Jim Finks's tenure as Saints general manager was a significant factor in his selection.

Retired numbers

- 31 Jim Taylor (officially retired, but is assigned to active players)
- 81 Doug Atkins (officially retired, but is assigned to active players)
- 51 Sam Mills (officially retired, but is assigned to active players)
- 57 Rickey Jackson (officially retired, but is assigned to active players)

New Orleans Saints Hall of Fame

The Saints Hall of Fame is a non-profit organization created by and for fans of the team to protect, preserve, promote and present the history of the franchise. The Saints Hall of Fame is located at 415 Williams Boulevard in the Rivertown section of Kenner. Open from 9 am-5 pm Tuesday through Saturday, the Hall of Fame features exhibits and memorabilia covering the entire history of the Saints from their formation through the current season. Due to building damage received during Hurricane Katrina the Hall of Fame is temporarily located at Gate B in the New Orleans Superdome and can be visited for free at every Saints home game. Fans can view videotapes on Saints history and the Saints Hall of Famers as well participate in interactive exhibits throughout the Hall. The facility, which originally opened on July 16, 1988, was expanded to twice its' original size in January 2004. Busts and paintings of each of the inductees along with their career highlights are one of the focal points of the museum, which is dedicated to preserving the history of the Saints franchise. New Orleans and Green Bay are the only two NFL franchises with a team Hall of Fame facility.

- 1988 QB Archie Manning, WR Danny Abramowicz
- 1989 S Tommy Myers, K Tom Dempsey
- 1990 QB Billy Kilmer
- 1991 NT Derland Moore, RB Tony Galbreath
- 1992 RB George Rogers, G Jake Kupp, C John Hill
- 1993 LB Joe Federspiel
- 1994 GM Jim Finks, TE Henry Childs
- 1995 DE Bob Pollard, DE Doug Atkins
- 1996 CB Dave Whitsell, DB Dave Waymer
- 1997 LB Rickey Jackson, T Stan Brock

- 1998 RB Dalton Hilliard, LB Sam Mills
- 1999 QB Bobby Hebert, WR Eric Martin
- 2000 LB Vaughan Johnson, LB Pat Swilling
- 2001 TE Hoby Brenner, DE Jim Wilks
- 2002 Coach Jim Mora, DE Frank Warren
- 2003 DE Wayne Martin, G/T Jim Dombrowski
- 2004 RB Rueben Mayes, Assistant Coach Steve Sidwell
- 2005–2006 C Joel Hilgenberg (2005 induction ceremonies postponed to October 27, 2006, due to Hurricane Katrina)
- 2007 DE Joe Johnson
- 2008 OT Willie Roaf
- 2009 K Morten Andersen
- 2010 WR Joe Horn

Joe Gemelli "Fleur-De-Lis" Award

Awarded yearly to a person who has contributed to the betterment of the New Orleans Saints organization.

- 1989: Al Hirt
- 1990: Joe Gemelli
- 1991: Dave Dixon
- 1992: Charlie Kertz
- 1993: Wayne Mack
- 1994: Erby Aucoin
- 1995: Aaron Broussard
- 1996: Marie Knutson
- 1997: Angela Hill
- 1998: Joe Impastato
- 1999: Frank Wilson
- 2000: Bob Remy
- 2001: Peter "Champ" Clark
- 2002: Dean Kleinschmidt
- 2003: Jim Fast
- 2004: Bob Roesler
- 2005–06: Bernard "Buddy" Diliberto (2005 induction ceremonies postponed to October 27, 2006 due to Hurricane Katrina)*
- 2007: New Orleans Saints fans
- 2008: Barra Birrcher

- 2009: Jerry Romig
- 2010: Dan "Chief" Simmons and Glennon "Silky" Powell

New Orleans Saints head coaches

Radio and television

The Saints' flagship station is WWL 870AM (FM Simulcast on WWL 105.3FM), one of the oldest radio stations in the city of New Orleans and one of the nation's most powerful as a clear-channel station with 50,000 watts of power. Jim Henderson and Hokie Gajan form the broadcast team. Most preseason games are televised on Cox Sports Television and WVUE (Channel 8), a station which has been owned by a consortium led by Saints owner Tom Benson since mid-2008. Tim Brando and Solomon Wilcots call the preseason action.

See also

- Occurrence of Religious Symbolism in U.S. Sports Team Names and Mascots

External links

- New Orleans Saints [1] Official Website

History of the Saints

History of the New Orleans Saints

This article is about the **history of the New Orleans Saints** NFL football team.

1960s

The city of New Orleans, Louisiana, was awarded an NFL franchise on November 1, 1967. In December John W. Mecom, Jr. became the majority shareholder and thus president of the team; later that month Tom Fears was named head coach. In December the team was named "Saints" due to its birthday on the Roman Catholic Church's All Saints Day--a fitting nickname for a team in the largely Catholic New Orleans area. The team's original stadium was Tulane Stadium, which could seat more than 80,000 fans. The team was placed in the Capitol Division of the NFL's Eastern Conference; their division foes were the Dallas Cowboys, Philadelphia Eagles, and Washington Redskins The team started off well, with a 5-1 pre-season record; then, on the first play of the regular season, wide receiver John Gilliam returned the opening kickoff 94 yards for a touchdown. However, this was not enough for the Saints and they lost their regular season opener to the Los Angeles Rams 27-13. Their first win came on November 5 as they defeated the Eagles 31-24. That would be one of the Saints' only triumphs in their inaugural campaign; they ended the season 3-11, the second-worst mark in the league and three-and-a-half games behind Washington in the divisional race. At the time, however, the Saints' 3 wins tied for the most ever for an expansion team's inaugural season.

Their next few seasons continued along similar lines. They improved slightly in 1968, putting up a 4-9-1 record as they competed in the Century Division against the Cleveland Browns, St. Louis Cardinals, and Pittsburgh Steelers; in 1969 they returned to the Capitol Division (featuring the same opponents as 1967) and managed to go 5-9.

1970-74

The 1970 season saw yet another realignment for the Saints due to the AFL-NFL merger. The Saints were placed in the NFC West, where they would remain through the 2001 NFL season. Their original NFC West competitors—the Atlanta Falcons, the Los Angeles (and later, St. Louis) Rams, and the San Francisco 49ers—would also remain in the division through 2001 (with the Carolina Panthers joining in the 1995 NFL season), leading to the development of long standing rivalries.

The season started off poorly for the Saints. After going 1-5-1 in the first seven games, Fears was fired and replaced by J.D. Roberts on November 3. In Roberts's first game as coach, New Orleans trailed the Detroit Lions 17-16 with time winding down, but Tom Dempsey kicked an NFL-record 63-yard field goal to win the game. Dempsey's achievement is made all the more remarkable by the fact that he was born without toes on his right foot (which he kicked with). This Saints victory, however, would be the last for the season; they lost their next 6 games to finish 2-11-1, the worst record in the young history of the franchise.

In the 1971 NFL Draft, the Saints owned the second overall pick behind the Boston Patriots. They selected Archie Manning from Ole Miss. In the season opener, Manning did not disappoint; he passed for 218 yards and a touchdown and ran in another touchdown on the final play to give the Saints a 24-20 win over the Rams. Four weeks later, Manning engineered a 24-14 upset of the Dallas Cowboys, the same Cowboys who would return to Tulane Stadium three months later and win Super Bowl VI over the Miami Dolphins. Throughout the season Manning split the quarterbacking duties with veteran Edd Hargett. Manning ended the season with six passing touchdowns and four rushing touchdowns; he did well enough to become the team's undisputed starter the next season. Despite the promise Manning showed, the Saints's misfortunes continued as they finished 4-8-2.

In 1972 the Saints started 0-5 and finished 2-11-1. During the 1973 preseason, the Saints fired Roberts and hired John North, who led the Saints to consecutive 5-9 seasons in 1973 and 1974.

1975-79

In 1975 the Saints moved from Tulane Stadium into the Louisiana Superdome. Despite the new stadium, they went just 2-12; North was fired after six games and Ernie Hefferle was named interim head coach for the final eight games of the season.

For the 1976 season, Hank Stram was hired as head coach; he came with a proven track record (three AFL titles, one Super Bowl win) from his years with the Kansas City Chiefs (formerly the Dallas Texans). However, his talents proved ineffective in his first season as the Saints went 4-10; Manning was sidelined the entire season after undergoing elbow surgery just after Stram's hiring, forcing the quarterback duties to be split by backup Bobby Scott and Chicago Bears castoff Bobby Douglass. 1977 was not much better as the Saints went 3-11, including a humiliating 33-14 loss to the Tampa Bay Buccaneers on December 11, the Bucs' first victory in the NFL after 26 consecutive losses.

In 1978 Stram was replaced by Dick Nolan. The season saw an improvement in the Saints' fortunes; Manning had the best season of his career up to that point, passing for 3,416 yards and 17 touchdowns. He was named to the NFC Pro Bowl squad for the first time and was also named the NFC's Most Valuable Player by The Sporting News and UPI. The Saints put together a record of 7-9, their best ever mark. The Saints might have made the playoffs if not had been for a pair of losses to the hated Atlanta Falcons where the Falcons used the "Big Ben" play to score the winning touchdown in the final seconds of each contest, as well as a last-minute loss to the eventual World Champion Pittsburgh

Steelers.

In 1979 the Saints built on the success of the previous year. After an 0-3 start (including a 40-34 overtime loss to the Falcons on opening day), the Saints won five of their next six games to take sole possession of the NFC West lead after nine games. The Saints were 7-6 heading into a Monday night game with the Oakland Raiders; their rivals for the NFC West title, the Rams, were 8-6. The Saints jumped out to a 35-14 lead and seemed certain to gain a share of first place with their win. But the Saints blew the lead and lost 42-35. The next week they were blown out 35-0 at the Superdome by the San Diego Chargers, ending their playoff hopes. The Saints, however, did manage to beat the Super Bowl-bound Rams (playing their last game at the Los Angeles Memorial Coliseum) in the last game of the regular season. This gave them an 8-8 record, the first non-losing season in team history.

1980-1985

In 1980, the Saints had high hopes after their two relatively successful seasons. However, the season was a miserable failure. The team started 0-12 and Dick Nolan was fired; he was replaced by Dick Stanfel, who lost two games before the Saints managed to win their game against the New York Jets, who finished with the league's second worst record at 4-12, by a point. The Saints then lost their last game of the season to the New England Patriots to finish 1-15, the worst mark in team history and (at the time) the worst for a 16-game schedule, since eclipsed by the 2008 Detroit Lions (0-16). A local journalist and radio/TV personality, Buddy Diliberto, wore a paper grocery bag over his head to promote the brown bag special of Sonic, the Saint's sponsor at the time. Many fans took to wearing bags over their heads when attending games. The moniker "Aints" was also born due to the ineptitude of the 1980 Saints.

In 1981 Bum Phillips was named head coach. The dismal 1980 season meant that the Saints would get the first pick in the 1981 NFL Draft. They selected Heisman-winning running back George Rogers out of South Carolina. Rogers was the team's workhorse, playing in all but one game and averaging more than 25 carries a game. He ran for a total of 1,674 yards, making him the NFL rushing champion. However, his fine performances were not enough to make the Saints a winning club. They finished the season 4-12, but two of those wins came over the Rams, New Orleans' first regular-season sweep of the Rams since the two teams were placed in the NFC West by the AFL-NFL merger in 1970.

In 1982 the Saints signed former Oakland Raiders and Houston Oilers quarterback Ken Stabler and traded Archie Manning to the Oilers. Two games into the season the Saints were 1-1, but a strike by the players led to the cancellation of seven games. When the season resumed, the Saints won two games in a row to take their record to 3-1, but they lost four games in a row before winning their last game. They finished 4-5, but missed out on qualifying for the playoffs (expanded to 16 teams due to the strike) on a tiebreaker.

1983 saw the Saints improve on the previous season once again. They hovered at or above .500 for most of the season, but lost a golden opportunity to stay one step ahead in the playoff race by giving up

17 points in the fourth quarter of a 31-28 loss to the New York Jets on *Monday Night Football*.Their playoff hopes came down to the final game of the season, when they hosted the Rams. Los Angeles scored two touchdowns on interception returns and another on a punt return, and Mike Lansford kicked a 42-yard field goal with six seconds remaining to give the Rams the victory and a playoff berth and end the Saints' season. The Saints finished 8-8, tying their previous best season record.

Eight weeks after the conclusion of the 1983 season, the Saints traded their number one pick in the 1984 NFL Draft to the New York Jets for quarterback Richard Todd, who had worn out his welcome in the Big Apple by throwing too many interceptions and was being phased out in favor of rookie Ken O'Brien. During the 1984 season, New Orleans traded for former Heisman Trophy winner and future Pro Football Hall of Fame running back Earl Campbell, who won the NFL rushing championship in each of his first three seasons with the Houston Oilers, when Bum Phillips coached the club. The Saints won for the first time on *Monday Night Football* by defeating the Pittsburgh Steelers in the Superdome, but a three-game losing streak late in the season dropped the Saints to 7-9.

The biggest news of the 1984 season was that John Mecom, the owner of the team for almost 20 years, was putting them up for sale. Speculation was rife that a new owner might move the Saints out of New Orleans, namely Jacksonville, Florida. But on May 31, 1985, negotiations were finalized to sell the team to Tom Benson, a native New Orleanian who owned numerous car dealerships throughout the New Orleans area. The team's future in New Orleans was safe for the time being.

In 1985 the Saints started off 3-2 but then lost six games in a row. Bum Phillips resigned twelve games into the season, and his son Wade Phillips, the Saints' defensive coordinator, was named interim coach. The Saints ended the season 5-11. A bright spot of the campaign was the emergence of Louisiana native Bobby Hebert at quarterback, who led the Saints to victories over the Vikings and Rams late in the season. Hebert previously spent three seasons in the United States Football League with the Michigan Panthers and Oakland Invaders, leading the Panthers to the first USFL championship in 1983.

Jim Mora era: 1986-1996

Before the 1986 season Benson put his stamp on the team by making two important hires: first, he named Jim Finks president and general manager; then, he named Jim Mora head coach. The Saints' offense struggled throughout the year after Hebert went down with a knee injury in the third game of the season, but behind a revitalized defense and NFC Rookie of the Year Rueben Mayes, New Orleans improved to 7-9.

The 1987 Saints started 1-1; then, another player strike. This time, however, replacement players were used until the regular players ended their strike. As a result, the season was only one game shorter than usual. The Saints went 2-1 with replacement players as they were led by their quarterback, New Orleans native John Fourcade. When the regular players returned, their first game was against the San Francisco 49ers. The Saints lost 24-22, but that would be the last time they would taste defeat that year.

They ran off a nine-game winning streak to close out the season--a remarkable feat considering that the Saints had never before won nine games in a season, let alone nine games in a row. The loss against San Francisco, however, would keep the Saints from being NFC West Champions; instead, the Saints finished 12-3, behind the 13-2 49ers, and had to settle for a wild-card spot in the playoffs despite having a better record than either of the other division champions that year. The Saints hosted the Minnesota Vikings on January 3, 1988; after twenty years, the Saints would finally take part in the NFL playoffs. The game started well for the Saints as they took a 7-0 lead, but Minnesota answered by taking a 31-10 lead into the half. The Vikings added 13 more points in the 2nd half to make the final score 44-10. Despite the loss, the Saints were recognized for their accomplishments; six players were selected for the Pro Bowl and Mora and Finks were named NFL Coach and Executive of the Year, respectively.

The 1988 Saints looked to return to the playoffs. After starting the season with a loss to their nemesis, the 49ers, the Saints bounced back with a seven-game win streak. After the streak, though, the Saints lost five of their next seven games. They won their last game of the season (against Atlanta), but they missed out on the playoffs due to tiebreakers.

The 1989 Saints managed to finish 9-7, but thanks to other strong performances in the NFC they missed the playoffs by two games.

In 1990 the Saints started off poorly, going 2-5 in their first seven games. However, they turned their season around and close wins in their final two games of the season were enough to give them an 8-8 record and a playoff berth in the newly expanded NFL playoffs, which now included six teams from each conference. They traveled to Soldier Field to take on the Chicago Bears, but lost 16-6.

In 1991 the Saints started with a seven-game win streak, opening up a four-game lead over the rest of the division. But then the Saints lost five of their next seven games, giving Atlanta and San Francisco a shot at claiming the division title. However, the Saints regrouped in the final two games of the season, and they finished 11-5 as the Falcons and 49ers finished 10-6 to give the Saints their first-ever division title. The Saints' first-round playoff game would be at the Superdome against Atlanta. The Falcons came from behind to defeat the Saints 27-20.

In 1992 the Saints attempted to defend their division title, but their hated rivals the 49ers swept the season series and finished 14-2 to the Saints' 12-4, meaning that the Saints would once again have to settle for a wild card berth to the NFC playoffs. They hosted the Philadelphia Eagles but once again could not put their home field advantage to good use, losing 36-20 for their fourth playoff loss in as many games.

The 1993 season would see the Saints start their decline from regular playoff contender to league doormat once again. They started off 5-0 but lost eight of their last eleven games to finish 8-8, one game out of the playoffs.

After seven straight years without a losing record, the returned to the losing ways of the pre-Mora era in 1994. The Saints started 4-8 on their way to a 7-9 record.

In 1995 the Saints again finished 7-9 in the NFC West, which was newly expanded to include the Carolina Panthers. Due to tiebreakers, the Saints had the disgrace of finishing in last place in the division behind even the expansion team.

In 1996, after the Saints started 2-6, Mora resigned after more than ten years with the franchise. He finished his Saints tenure with 93 wins and 78 losses, making him far and away the most successful Saints coach ever--in fact, the only one (up to then) ever to have a winning record during his Saints tenure. Rick Venturi was named interim head coach, but he had even less success than Mora did that season, going 1-7 to bring the Saints' final record to 3-13, their worst record since 1980.

The Ditka era: 1997-99

Before the 1997 season Tom Benson named legendary Chicago Bears coach Mike Ditka as the Saints coach, leading to optimism that he would be able to win a Super Bowl with the Saints as he had done with the Bears. However, the Ditka era would be a tumultuous time for the organization.

In 1997 Ditka led the team to a 6-10 record, a three-game improvement from the previous season; the team was marked by strong defense (anchored by defensive end Joe Johnson, middle linebacker Winfred Tubbs, and veteran cornerback Eric Allen, among others) and inconsistent offense.

The 1998 season was even more chaotic. Starting quarterback Billy Joe Hobert was lost for the year in the season-opening win against the St. Louis Rams. Later in the season, the team claimed quarterback Kerry Collins off the waiver wire; Collins had been released by the Carolina Panthers earlier in the season after he informed the team his heart wasn't in the game anymore. Collins was inconsistent as a starter, including a 31-17 loss to a previously winless Panthers team, but he was also at the helm for a 22-3 upset of the Dallas Cowboys, the high point of the season, before being benched against the Buffalo Bills in week 17. His lackluster performance, coupled with a highly publicized DUI arrest, led Ditka to state that the team would not seek to re-sign Collins. The Saints finished 6-10 once again.

In the months before the 1999 NFL Draft, Ditka became enamored with Texas running back Ricky Williams, the Heisman Trophy winner who'd set an NCAA record for career rushing yards with the Longhorns. Ditka's remarks that he'd "trade his entire draft" for the standout runner were well-publicized; holding the #13 overall pick, the Saints would need to trade up to have a chance at selecting Williams.

They got their chance to do so when the Indianapolis Colts selected Miami running back Edgerrin James with the #4 overall pick. The Saints orchestrated a three-way trade with the Washington Redskins and the Chicago Bears that involved the Saints' taking Washington's #5 overall pick — and, therefore, Williams — in exchange for all the Saints' remaining 1999 draft picks *and* their first- and third-rounders in 2000.

The trade drew mixed reactions from Saints fans. In the days after the draft, Ditka boldly predicted that the Saints would go to the Super Bowl.

Fan opinion began to solidify against Ditka when it became clear that his prediction would not come true. The Saints' 1999 season was marked by yet more inconsistency at quarterback, a porous defense, and a hobbled Williams, who struggled with a high ankle sprain and an elbow injury in his rookie year. The Saints finished 3-13. Owner Tom Benson had had enough; soon after the season ended, he fired Ditka, the entire coaching staff, and general manager Bill Kuharich.

The Ditka era in New Orleans saw seven different starters at quarterback in three seasons (Heath Shuler, Danny Wuerffel, Doug Nussmeier, Billy Joe Hobert, Billy Joe Tolliver, Kerry Collins, and Jake Delhomme) and a defense which went from top-ten to near the bottom of the league in nearly every statistical category.

2000-present

To replace Ditka and Kuharich, Benson settled on Randy Mueller, formerly of the Seattle Seahawks, as general manager, and Pittsburgh Steelers defensive coordinator Jim Haslett as head coach. Mueller shook up the roster, bringing in a squad of fresh talent via free agency: wide receivers Jake Reed and Joe Horn, quarterback Jeff Blake, tight end Andrew Glover, defensive tackle Norman Hand, cornerback Fred Thomas, safety Chris Oldham, and linebacker Darrin Smith, among others. Lacking their top draft pick because of the Williams trade (a pick the Redskins would use to draft linebacker LaVar Arrington), New Orleans selected defensive end Darren Howard early in the second round.

Inspired by Terrell Davis and the Denver Broncos offense, new offensive coordinator Mike McCarthy implemented a form of the West Coast Offense with Ricky Williams as the focal point: a run-first attack designed to open up passing lanes and create opportunities for the occasional deep ball.

After a sputtering 1-3 start, the Saints found their groove, winning six straight games behind Williams and an opportunistic defense. The season marked the surprising emergence of Joe Horn, who'd previously been a backup receiver with the Kansas City Chiefs but was flourishing as Blake's main target.

Adversity struck, however, with injuries in consecutive games to Williams and Blake, forcing the team to rely on backups at both positions for the remainder of the season. Blake's injury presented an opportunity for quarterback Aaron Brooks, who led the team to two critical road wins: an upset over the defending-champion St. Louis Rams and a late comeback against the San Francisco 49ers, keeping the Saints atop the NFC West. A Week 16 victory over the Atlanta Falcons, coupled with a St. Louis loss the following night, gave the Saints a 10-5 record, a playoff berth, and their first division title since 1991.

In the regular season finale the Saints lost to the Rams, setting up a rematch between the two teams in the wild-card playoff round. Though they lost Horn to an injury early in the game, the Saints managed to surge ahead to a 31-7 lead early in the fourth quarter behind three touchdowns from Brooks to backup wide receiver Willie Jackson. A late comeback by the Rams was halted in dramatic fashion when St. Louis wide receiver Az-Zahir Hakim fumbled a punt late in the game. Saints fullback Brian Milne fell on the ball and the Saints were able to run out the clock to secure their first-ever playoff win. The final score was 31-28.

The return of Ricky Williams the next week could not prevent the injury-hobbled Saints from losing to the Minnesota Vikings. Despite the loss, the 2000 season was viewed as an overwhelming success by the fans and the media. Haslett and Mueller were recognized by the league as Coach of the Year and Executive of the Year, respectively. Five Saints were selected to the Pro Bowl: Horn, left tackle Willie Roaf, defensive linemen Joe Johnson and La'Roi Glover, and linebacker Keith Mitchell. Horn set a franchise record with 1,340 receiving yards and emerged as a playmaker and tenacious possession receiver. Despite his injury, Williams rushed for 1,000 yards and eight touchdowns in 10 games.

The seasons following 2000 have failed to meet the raised expectations of fans and media. The 2001 season established a trend of team inconsistency from week to week: though the Saints engineered a stirring comeback from several touchdowns down to beat the Rams on the road, they also collapsed at the end of the season, losing their last four games by embarrassing margins to finish 7-9.

The season was notable for the curious behavior of Albert Connell, a wide receiver acquired in the offseason and intended to be the long-term starter opposite Joe Horn. Connell was accused of, and subsequently admitted to, stealing over $4,000 from teammate Deuce McAllister, though he claimed the theft was just a prank. Connell caught only 12 passes in 11 games with the Saints; the team suspended him for the last four games of the season and later terminated his contract.

In the offseason, the Saints — having drafted running back Deuce McAllister in the first round of the 2001 NFL Draft — traded starter Ricky Williams to the Miami Dolphins. The trade ended up giving the Saints two first-round picks.

2002

The 2002 season started with promise but finished in familiar fashion. The Saints began the year with impressive wins over three 2001 playoff teams — an overtime win over new division rival Tampa Bay, a 15-point trouncing of Green Bay, and a come-from-behind win over Chicago on the road. But the season would include a loss to bottom-dweller Detroit, as well as another late-season collapse that included three straight losses to Minnesota, Cincinnati, and Carolina, when a victory in any one of these three games would have all but guaranteed a playoff berth. The Saints, after starting 6-1, would finish at 9-7 and would miss the playoffs once again.

Haslett and the coaching staff drew criticism for not benching starter Aaron Brooks in any of the season's final games. Brooks had been hobbled by a shoulder injury, and though both he and Haslett insisted the injury would not affect his play, the quarterback's performance suggested otherwise. Over the last six games of the season, Brooks completed only 47% of his passes, throwing for six touchdowns and five interceptions and losing six fumbles. His passer rating over those six games was 66.7, far less than his 80.1 rating over the entire season.

Backing up Brooks in 2002 was fan-favorite Jake Delhomme, who'd played at nearby UL-Lafayette and had come off the bench to cement a victory over Tampa Bay several weeks earlier. Brooks' poor performance late in the 2002 season prompted fans to chant "We Want Jake!" at games, but Haslett ignored these chants. In the offseason Delhomme signed with Carolina, in part because he'd be able to compete for the starting job. Delhomme would lead the Panthers to Super Bowl XXXVIII in his first season with the Panthers, further rubbing salt in the wounds of Saints fans.

2003

The 2003 season started off poorly for the Saints, going 1-4 in their first five games, including a 55-21 blowout loss at home against the Indianapolis Colts as Colts quarterback and New Orleans native Peyton Manning threw six touchdown passes to hand the Saints a humiliating loss on national television. The Saints, however, would rebound somewhat from their poor start and finish the season 8-8. McAllister ran for a career-high 1,641 yards.

2004

The 2004 season saw the Saints struggle out of the gate. They compiled a 4-8 record in their first twelve games and Haslett's job appeared to be in jeopardy. Then the Saints put together three straight wins (two of them on the road) to give them a shot at an 8-8 record and a playoff berth. The Saints faced Carolina (also 7-8) in Week 17. The Saints would need to beat the Panthers; they would also need one of two things to happen: a St. Louis tie or loss; or a Seattle win or tie and a Minnesota win or tie. The New Orleans, St. Louis, and Minnesota games were all played at 1 p.m. EST that Sunday of Week 17. The Saints defeated the Panthers 21-18 but Minnesota lost to Washington (by a 21-18 score, oddly enough), meaning that the Saints' playoff chances came down to the game between the Rams and the Jets. The game went to overtime with the score tied at 29. The teams battled back and forth for most of the overtime period. The crucial moment occurred when Jets kicker Doug Brien (formerly of the Saints) missed a 53-yard field goal. The Rams capitalized on the good field position and kicked a field goal of their own to win with just a little over 3 minutes left in overtime, sending the Saints out of the playoffs on the tiebreaker scenarios. Though the Saints had beaten the Rams earlier in the season, their loss to the Vikings and the fact that the Rams did not play the Vikings that season meant that the tiebreaker had to go to best conference record, where the Rams finished ahead of the Saints and Vikings to claim one of the NFC's wild card spots. The Vikings then got the final wild card spot thanks to their win over the Saints. While the season finished in heartbreaking fashion, many thought that Haslett would have been fired if not for his team's four game win streak to end the season.

2005

Going into the 2005 season the Saints were optimistic that they could build on their good results at the end of 2004. But when Hurricane Katrina struck, the Saints were thrown into chaos with the rest of their city. The Saints relocated their headquarters to San Antonio, Texas. The Saints managed to provide an emotional lift for their hometown when they defeated the Panthers 23-20 in Week 1. The NFL decreed that the Saints' first home game would be played in Giants Stadium, adding insult to injury as the Saints were forced to play a "home" game in front of a hostile crowd. Due to a Jets game scheduled for Giants Stadium that Sunday, the Saints played in a unique Monday Night Football doubleheader, with the game starting at 7:30 EDT on ABC before the regularly scheduled game, with the Saints and Giants moving to ESPN (except in New Orleans and New York) when the second game started. The Saints struggled and lost 27-10, feeling aggrieved at the situation. The rest of the Saints home games would be played either in San Antonio's Alamodome or Baton Rouge's Tiger Stadium. The Saints lost to Minnesota in Week 3 but won in the Alamodome the next week over Buffalo to bring their record 2-2. They then proceeded to be blown out 52-3 in Green Bay by a team which came into the game 0-4. The Green Bay loss was even worse for the Saints due to the season-ending injury suffered by star RB Deuce McAllister. The Saints would eventually finish the season with a 3-13 record; the last few games of the season saw quarterback Aaron Brooks being benched (and later traded to the Oakland Raiders), playing time for backup quarterback Todd Bouman and even third-stringer Adrian McPherson and, eventually, the season ended with head coach Jim Haslett losing his job.

2006

The 2006 Saints orchestrated one of the more remarkable turnarounds in NFL history, as they were the first team to go from 3-13 to a conference title game the next season. First year coach Sean Payton, who came from Dallas as a Bill Parcells pupil, was hired for a daunting task at hand. In his first move as coach, he released almost half of the roster, most notably inconsistent QB Aaron Brooks.

The Saints were aggressive in free agency, signing former San Diego Chargers QB Drew Brees, who was coming off of orthopedic surgery. Brees nearly played for the Miami Dolphins, but the team's doctors doubted whether Drew's arm could recover in time for the season. The Saints gambled on Drew's ability to recover in time for the season and signed him to a major long term contract. Then came April, and the 2006 NFL Draft.

On the eve before the draft on April 29th, news broke that the Houston Texans could not reach an agreement with Reggie Bush and instead reached a deal with Mario Williams as the #1 pick. When the team found out that Reggie would be available, they selected the USC running back with their #2 pick. In that draft the Saints also picked a player who would become a standout from the 7th round: Marques Colston from Hofstra as the 252nd pick.

When preseason got underway the Saints started out strong in a victory over the Tennessee Titans, which featured a dazzling run by Reggie Bush where he reversed his direction for a big run. That was the only highlight for the Saints preseason as they finished just 1-3, losing their next 3 preseason games.

The season officially began for the Saints with a road win against the Cleveland Browns, with Bush accounting for 129 yards from scrimmage, while Marques Colston caught a TD pass from Brees. The next week the Saints went to Green Bay, where the Saints lost 52-3 the previous year, to face the Packers. The start of the game looked bleak for the Saints as they quickly went down 13-0, but Drew Brees led a comeback, throwing for 353 yards and two TDs as the Saints came back to win a shootout 34-27. The Saints were then headed back for the first game in the Superdome since the 2005 preseason, a Monday Night date with the Atlanta Falcons on September 25th.

The Saints entered the game 2-0 against the 2-0 Falcons with many expecting the Falcons powerful running game to overwhelm the team. The game kicked off to fanfare of the Saints' official return to New Orleans. The game also featured pregame festivities featuring Green Day and U2 performing a song that would become the team's unofficial anthem, "The Saints are Coming". New Orleans dominated the game right from the start when Steve Gleason blocked a punt that was recovered for a TD by Curtis Deloatch. The Saints went on to win 23-3.

The next week the Saints lost their first game of the season to divisional rival Carolina Panthers 18-21. The team bounced back in their second game in New Orleans facing divisional rival Tampa Bay. In the game with time winding down and the Saints down by 4 the Saints were set to receive a punt. Reggie Bush returned the punt 65 yards, untouched, for the winning touchdown, and the first of his career. The Saints were 4-1 and in control of the division. A week later the Saints upset the favored Eagles in New Orleans 27-24, and the Saints were taken seriously heading into their bye week.

New Orleans entered a midseason slump, losing 3 of 4 by week 10 before going on a three-game win streak. They defeated Atlanta, San Francisco, and Dallas in convincing fashion.

The Saints concluded the regular season at 10-6, winning the divisional title and, for the first time in the team's history, securing a first-round bye in the playoffs.

The Saints' divisional bout would be a week 6 rematch with the Eagles, who were led by backup QB Jeff Garcia this time and riding a six-game winning streak. The game featured several lead changes and a most inspired effort by Deuce McAllister, who rushed for almost 150 yards and 2 TDs, 1 receiving and 1 rushing. New Orleans would win its first divisional playoff game in team history 27-24 against the Eagles, and only the second playoff win in franchise history. The Saints then traveled to Chicago to face the Bears in the team's first-ever NFC Championship appearance, where they ended up falling short in the title game 39-14.

New Orleans led the league in total yards gained and passing yards in the 2006 season. Drew Brees set new Saints' single-season records in passes completed (356), passing rating (96.2) and passing yards (4,418). The team sent three players to the 2007 Pro Bowl: the aforementioned Brees, DE Will Smith and LT Jammal Brown

2007-2008

The 2007 regular season began with a prime time match against the defending champion Colts, but New Orleans suffered a 41-10 pounding. The losses continued as Tampa Bay and Tennessee routed them, followed by a close loss to Carolina. The Saints finally managed a victory in Week 6 by defeated Seattle 28-17. After three more victories, they lost two, beat Carolina, and then fell to the Buccaneers again. The Week 16 defeat against Philadelphia removed New Orleans from playoff contention. After a final loss to the Bears, they ended with a 7-9 record.

In 2008, the Saints began by defeating their division rival Buccaneers before losing three of the next four matches. New Orleans was selected for that year's international series game in London, where they beat San Diego 37-32. The remainder of the season was an uneven string of games, and after beating Carolina on December 28, the team ended its 2008 campaign with an 8-8 record.

2009 - The road to the Super Bowl

New Orleans started off 2009 innocently enough with a rout of the hapless Detroit Lions. Afterwards, they traveled to Philadelphia and beat an Eagles team that was missing its quarterback Donovan McNabb due to injuries. The Saints won with a score very close to the one in the Detroit game. They accumulated further easy wins over the Bills and Jets in the next two games. After the bye week, they handily defeated the Giants and then took the Dolphins at Landshark Stadium. In the second half, the Saints overcame an early lead by their opponent. With this impressive win, they moved to 6-0. The next four opponents were comparatively weak ones, and the Saints soon found themselves at 10-0 along with the Colts. In Week 12, they faced New England in the Superdome and inflicted a stunning defeat on the three-time Super Bowl champions. The next game however, the Saints nearly lost it as they played the 3-8 Redskins in Fedex Field. The score was tied at 30-30 when the fourth quarter ended, and in overtime Washington almost broke their eleven-game winning streak. However, a missed field goal prevented this from happening and the Saints regained possession of the ball. They kicked a successful FG, and won the game 33-30. Afterwards, New Orleans faced the Cowboys at home and were finally brought down, the score being 24-17. After that, they lost their final two matches against Tampa Bay and Carolina to end the regular season at 13-3. They had secured the division title and the #1 NFC seed after the Redskins game, and so rested up during the wild card round of the playoffs. The reenergized team came back from their bye week and hosted the Arizona Cardinals, crushing them 45-14. Now in the conference championship, the Saints faced the Vikings. The two teams waged an epic struggle through all four quarters. Minnesota QB Brett Favre was hit several times by the New Orleans defensive line and there were multiple penalties, timeouts, and booth reviews of questionable plays. Although the Vikings never trailed by more than a touchdown, they could not gain a lead and as the fourth quarter was drawing to a close, Favre threw an ill-advised pass across the middle which was intercepted by Saints cornerback Tracey Porter. The game went into overtime and New Orleans got possession of the ball after winning the coin toss. They finally kicked a 38-yard FG, sending them to

Super Bowl XLIV.

The Super Bowl was played in Miami against the Colts, who had won SB XLI there three years earlier. Indianapolis gained an early lead and the score stood at 10-0 to start the second quarter. The Saints were unable to obtain a touchdown and instead went for two long field goals. By halftime, the score was 10-6. The third quarter opened with New Orleans making a surprise onside kick, and both teams got into an argument over who got hold of the ball. The Saints were ultimately ruled to have touched it first. A screen pass by Drew Brees to Pierre Thomas made for a successful touchdown, increasing their lead to 13-10. After another Colts touchdown, the Saints kicked another FG to achieve a 17-16 score. The game remained close into the fourth quarter until Colts QB Peyton Manning was intercepted by Tracey Porter and his pass returned for a touchdown. A strong defensive effort by New Orleans halted their opponent's attempts at another scoring drive, and the game ended 31-17. The Saints had finally won a championship after decades of futility, sending the city of New Orleans into wild celebrations.

References

- http://www.neworleanssaints.com/custompage.cfm?pageid=66
- http://www.profootballhof.com/history/team.jsp?franchise_id=20
- http://www.sportsecyclopedia.com/nfl/norleans/saints.html
- http://www.pro-football-reference.com/teams/norindex.htm

List of New Orleans Saints seasons

This is a list of **seasons completed by the New Orleans Saints American football franchise** of the National Football League (NFL). The list documents the season-by-season records of the Saints' franchise from to present, including postseason records, and league awards for individual players or head coaches.

- *Note: The Finish, Wins, Losses, and Ties columns list regular season results and exclude any postseason play. Italicized numbers mean that the records are subject to change each week due to regular season or postseason games being played.*

Super Bowl Champions (1970–present)	Conference Champions	Division Champions	Wild Card Berth	League Leader

Season	Team	League	Conference	Division	Regular Season				Postseason Results	Awards
					Finish	Wins	Losses	Ties		
	1967	NFL	Eastern	Capitol	4th	3	11	0		
	1968	NFL	Eastern	Century	3rd	4	9	1		
	1969	NFL	Eastern	Capitol	3rd	5	9	0		
AFL-NFL Merger										
	1970	NFL	NFC	West	4th	2	11	1		
	1971	NFL	NFC	West	4th	4	8	2		
	1972	NFL	NFC	West	4th	2	11	1		
	1973	NFL	NFC	West	3rd	5	9	0		
	1974	NFL	NFC	West	3rd	5	9	0		
	1975	NFL	NFC	West	4th	2	12	0		
	1976	NFL	NFC	West	3rd	4	10	0		
	1977	NFL	NFC	West	4th	3	11	0		
	1978	NFL	NFC	West	3rd	7	9	0		Archie Manning (Sporting News NFL MVP, UPI NFC Off. POTY)
	1979	NFL	NFC	West	2nd	8	8	0		
	1980	NFL	NFC	West	4th	1	15	0		
	1981	NFL	NFC	West	4th	4	12	0		
	1982	NFL	NFC	West	9th[1]	4	5	0		
	1983	NFL	NFC	West	3rd	8	8	0		
	1984	NFL	NFC	West	3rd	7	9	0		
	1985	NFL	NFC	West	4th	5	11	0		
	1986	NFL	NFC	West	4th	7	9	0		

	1987	NFL	NFC	West	2nd	12	3	0	Lost Wild Card Playoffs (Vikings) 44-10	Jim Mora (NFL COY)
	1988	NFL	NFC	West	3rd	10	6	0		
	1989	NFL	NFC	West	3rd	9	7	0		
	1990	NFL	NFC	West	2nd	8	8	0	Lost Wild Card Playoffs (Bears) 16-6	
	1991	NFL	NFC	**West**	**1st**	11	5	0	Lost Wild Card Playoffs (Falcons) 27-20	Pat Swilling (NFL Def. POTY)
	1992	NFL	NFC	West	2nd	12	4	0	Lost Wild Card Playoffs (Eagles) 36-20	
	1993	NFL	NFC	West	2nd	8	8	0		
	1994	NFL	NFC	West	2nd	7	9	0		
	1995	NFL	NFC	West	5th	7	9	0		
	1996	NFL	NFC	West	5th	3	13	0		
	1997	NFL	NFC	West	3rd	6	10	0		
	1998	NFL	NFC	West	3rd	6	10	0		
	1999	NFL	NFC	West	5th	3	13	0		
	2000	NFL	NFC	**West**	**1st**	10	6	0	**Won** Wild Card Playoffs (Rams) 31-28 Lost Divisional Playoffs (Vikings) 34-16	Jim Haslett (NFL COY)
	2001	NFL	NFC	West	3rd	7	9	0		
	2002	NFL	NFC	South	3rd	9	7	0		
	2003	NFL	NFC	South	2nd	8	8	0		
	2004	NFL	NFC	South	2nd	8	8	0		
	2005	NFL	NFC	South	4th	3	13	0		

	2006	NFL	NFC	**South**	**1st**	10	6	0	**Won** Divisional Playoffs (Eagles) 27-24 Lost Conference Championship (Bears) 39-14	Sean Payton (NFL COY)
2007	2007	NFL	NFC	South	2nd	7	9	0		
	2008	NFL	NFC	South	4th	8	8	0		Drew Brees (NFL Off. POTY)
	2009	**NFL**	**NFC**	**South**	**1st**	13	3	0	**Won** Divisional Playoffs (Cardinals) 45-14 **Won** Conference Championship (Vikings) 31-28 **Won** Super Bowl **XLIV** (Colts) 31-17	Drew Brees (SB MVP)
Totals	275	378	5	**(1967–2009, includes only regular season)**						
5	6	-	**(1967–2009, includes only playoffs)**							
280	**384**	**5**	**(1967–2009, includes both regular season and playoffs)**							

[1] Due to a strike-shortened season in 1982, all teams were ranked by conference instead of division.

The Field

Louisiana Superdome

The **Louisiana Superdome** − often informally known as the **Superdome, The Dome** or the **New Orleans Superdome** − is a sports and exhibition facility located in the Central Business District of New Orleans, Louisiana. Plans were drawn up in 1967 by the New Orleans modernist architectural firm of Curtis and Davis, the company also responsible for design of the main branch of the New Orleans Public Library (1956–58).

The Superdome is home to the NFL's New Orleans Saints and the NCAA's Division I Tulane University football team. It is one of the few facilities in the United States which can host major sporting events such as the Super Bowl and the Final Four; as such, given New Orleans' popularity as a tourist destination, whenever the Superdome bids to host such an event it routinely makes the "short list" of candidates being considered. It has been chosen to host Super Bowl XLVII in February 2013.

The Superdome is the largest *fixed* domed structure in the world. Its steel frame covers a expanse. Its dome is made of a Lamella multi-ringed frame and has a diameter of .

In 2005, the Superdome came to international attention when it housed thousands of people seeking shelter from Hurricane Katrina, and it was damaged in the storm.

Capacity

The Superdome has a listed football seating capacity of 72,968 (expanded) or 69,703 (not expanded), a maximum basketball seating capacity of 55,675, and a maximum baseball capacity of 63,525; however, published attendance figures from events such as the Sugar Bowl football game have exceeded 85,000. A 1981 Rolling Stones concert attracted more than 87,500 spectators. The basketball capacity does not reflect the NCAA's new policy on arranging the basketball court on the 50-yard line on the football field, per 2009 NCAA policy.

Stadium history

Sports visionary David Dixon, (who decades later founded the United States Football League) conceived of the Superdome while attempting to convince the NFL to award a franchise to New Orleans. After hosting several exhibition games at Tulane Stadium during typical New Orleans summer thunderstorms, Dixon was told by NFL Commissioner Pete Rozelle that the NFL would never expand into New Orleans without a domed stadium. Dixon then won the support of the governor of Louisiana,

John McKeithen. When they toured the Astrodome in Houston, Texas in 1966, McKeithen was quoted as saying, "I want one of these, only bigger," in reference to the Astrodome itself. Bonds were passed for construction of the Superdome on November 8, 1966, seven days after commissioner Pete Rozelle awarded New Orleans the 25th professional football franchise. The stadium was conceptualized to be a multifunctional stadium but without consideration for professional baseball. Dixon imagined the possibilities of staging simultaneous high school football games side-by-side and suggested that the synthetic surface be white. Blount International of Montgomery, Alabama was chosen to build the stadium.

It was hoped the stadium would be ready in time for the 1972 NFL season, and the final cost of the facility would come in at $46 million. Instead, due to political delays, construction did not start until August 11, 1971 and was not finished until August 1975, seven months after Super Bowl IX was scheduled to be played in the stadium. Since the stadium was not finished in time for the Super Bowl, the game had to be moved to Tulane Stadium and was played in cold and rainy conditions. Factoring in inflation, construction delays, and the increase in transportation costs caused by the 1973 oil crisis, the final price tag of the stadium skyrocketed to $165 million. The first Super Bowl played in the stadium was Super Bowl XII in January 1978, the first in prime time.

The New Orleans Saints opened the 1975 NFL season at the Superdome, losing 21–0 to the Cincinnati Bengals in the first regular season game in the facility. Tulane Stadium was condemned on the day the Superdome opened, although the original concrete sections stood on the Tulane University campus until November 1979.

The Superdome is located on of land, including the former Girod Street Cemetery. The dome has an interior space of , a height of , a dome diameter of , and a total floor area of .

The New Orleans Arena, adjacent to the Louisiana Superdome, opened on October 19, 1999. A smaller conventional indoor arena, it was designed by Arthur Q. Davis, whose former firm had designed the Superdome.

The Superdome converted its artificial grass surface to Field Turf midway through the 2003 football season, replacing the original AstroTurf surface on November 16. After being damaged from the flooding of Hurricane Katrina in 2005, a new Sportexe MomentumTurf surface was installed for the 2006 season.

Baseball

The first baseball game in the Superdome was an exhibition between the Minnesota Twins and the Houston Astros on April 6, 1976. The American Association New Orleans Pelicans played at the Superdome during the 1977 season. The Pelicans' season attendance was 217,957 at the dome.

Superdome officials pursued negotiations with Oakland Athletics officials during the 1978-1979 baseball off-season about moving the Athletics to the Superdome. The Athletics were unable to break their lease at the Oakland-Alameda County Coliseum and remained in Oakland. Superdome officials met with the Pittsburgh Pirates in April 1981 about moving the club to New Orleans when the Pirates were unhappy with their lease at Three Rivers Stadium.

The New York Yankees played exhibition games at the Superdome in 1980, 1981, 1982, and 1983. The Yankees hosted the Baltimore Orioles on March 15 and 16, 1980. 45,152 spectators watched the Yankees beat the Orioles 9 to 3 on March 15, 1980. The following day, 43,339 fans saw Floyd Rayford lead the Orioles to a 7 to 1 win over the Yankees. Late in 1982, the Yankees considered opening the 1983 regular season at the Superdome if Yankee Stadium would not be ready yet after renovations. Attendance slipped to 15,129 for a March 27, 1983 Yankees-Blue Jays exhibition game at the Superdome. The Philadelphia Phillies and St. Louis Cardinals closed the 1984 spring training season with two games at the dome on March 31, 1984 and April 1, 1984.

Hurricane Katrina

Effect of Hurricane Katrina

The Superdome was used as a "shelter of last resort" for those in New Orleans unable to evacuate from Hurricane Katrina when it struck in late August 2005. During the storm, a large section of the outer covering was peeled off by high winds. The photos of the damage, in which the concrete underneath was exposed, quickly became an iconic image of Hurricane Katrina. A few days later the dome was closed until September 25, 2006. During the ordeal, the stadium sheltered about 30,000 people.

Reopening after Katrina

The Superdome cost $185 million to repair and refurbish. To repair the Superdome, FEMA put up $115 million, the state spent $13 million, the Louisiana Stadium & Expedition District refinanced a bond package to secure $41 million and the NFL contributed $15 million.

On Super Bowl XL Sunday (February 5, 2006), the NFL announced that the Saints would play their home opener on September 24, 2006 in the Superdome against the Atlanta Falcons. The game was later moved to Monday night, September 25, 2006.

The reopening of the dome was celebrated with festivities including a free outdoor concert by the Goo Goo Dolls before fans were allowed in, a pre-game performance by the rock bands U2 and Green Day performing a cover of The Skids' "The Saints Are Coming", and a coin toss conducted by former President George H. W. Bush. In front of ESPN's largest-ever audience at that time, the Saints won the game 23–3 with 70,003 in attendance and went on to a successful season reaching their first ever NFC Championship Game.

The first bowl game played in the Superdome after Katrina was the New Orleans Bowl won by the Troy University Trojans 41–17 over the Rice University Owls.

Renovations

The Superdome is scheduled to undergo $320 million in renovations in three phases, due to its contract with the New Orleans Saints. New windows have been installed for natural lighting, and an new face lift will be constructed. The roof-facing of the Superdome will have a solid white hue and the sides of the dome panels will resemble a champagne bronze color. The entire outer layer of the stadium, more than 400,000 square feet of aluminum siding, will be replaced with new aluminum panels and insulation, and an innovative barrier system for drainage will be added by 2010. The dome is set to resemble its original facade.

In addition, escalators will be added to the outside of the club rooms. Each suite will have modernized rooms with raised ceilings, leather sofas and flat-screen TVs, as well as glass, brushed aluminum and wood-grain furnishings. A new $600,000 point-of-sale system is also being installed, which will allow fans to purchase concessions with credit cards throughout the stadium for the first time. Once all three phases of the renovation are completed the Superdome will be one of the most up-to-date facilities in the U.S.

Major events

Annual sporting events

- Home games for the New Orleans Saints
- Home games for Tulane University college football
- Home to the Sugar Bowl since 1975 (except in 2006 when, due to Hurricane Katrina damage, the game was temporarily relocated to Atlanta), one of the four major college football bowl games (the Southeastern Conference champion is the host team unless it is selected to participate in the BCS National Championship Game)
- Home to the New Orleans Bowl since 2001 (except in 2005 when, due to Hurricane Katrina damage, the game was temporarily relocated to Lafayette), a minor bowl game featuring the Sun Belt Conference champion (as the host team; the Conference is headquartered in New Orleans) against a member of Conference USA
- Home to the Bayou Classic a Thanksgiving Day weekend college football game featuring Louisiana's two public historically black universities, Grambling State and Southern University.

- Home to the Louisiana high school football state championships

Rotating sporting events

The following major sporting events are those in which the Superdome is either on a rotating list of facilities to host the event, or is widely considered to be on a "short list" of facilities to host it:

- BCS National Championship Game – As the host site of the Sugar Bowl, the Superdome rotates with the locations of the other three major college bowl games (the Rose Bowl, Fiesta Bowl, and Orange Bowl) as the host for the BCS National Championship Game. The Superdome hosted the BCS National Championship Game in 2000, 2004, and 2008, and is scheduled to host the game again in 2012.
- Super Bowl – More Super Bowls have been played at the Louisiana Superdome than at any other sports facility: 1978, 1981, 1986, 1990, 1997, and 2002. The Superdome is currently scheduled to host the 2013 Super Bowl.
- The Final Four – the Superdome hosted the NCAA college basketball Final Fours in 1982, 1987, 1993, and 2003. The Superdome is scheduled to host the games again in 2012.

Other notable events

Sports

- 1980 – The infamous "No Mas" boxing match between Sugar Ray Leonard & Roberto Durán.
- 1994 – two spring training games between the Boston Red Sox and New York Yankees.
- January 24, 2010 - The Superdome hosted its first NFC Championship Game, which the Saints won 31-28 over the Minnesota Vikings in overtime.
- September 9, 2010 - The Superdome will host the 2010 NFL Kickoff game.

Wrestling

- Late 1970s/Early 1980s – Mid South Wrestling quarterly events
- April 19, 1986 – The first National Wrestling Alliance Jim Crockett Sr. Memorial Tag Team Tournament.
- April 2, 1989 – *Clash of the Champions VI* - WCW pay-per-view wrestling event

Concerts

- The Rolling Stones - *1978 North American Tour* - July 13, 1978, *1981 North American Tour* - December 5, 1981, *Steel Wheels Tour* - November 13, 1989 & *Voodoo Lounge Tour* - October 10, 1994
- David Bowie - *Glass Spider Tour* - October 6, 1987
- Aerosmith - *Pump Tour* - May 15, 1990
- Metallica & Guns N' Roses - *Guns N' Roses/Metallica Stadium Tour*, with Faith No More - July 29, 1992

- Paul McCartney - *The New World Tour* - April 24, 1993
- Pink Floyd - *The Division Bell Tour* - May 14, 1994
- January 13, 1997, January 19, 1998 & June 21, 1999 – WCW Monday Nitro shows.
- U2 - *PopMart Tour* - November 21, 1997
- Janet Jackson - *The Velvet Rope Tour*, with 'N Sync - October 28, 1998
- Cher - *Do You Believe? Tour* - June 23, 1999
- 'N Sync - *No Strings Attached Tour*, with Sisqo & P!nk - May 27, 2000 & *Pop Odyssey Tour* - August 22, 2001 (The concert was released on VHS & DVD in early 2002, titled *Pop Odyssey Live*.)
- Alicia Keys - *Songs in A Minor Tour* - July 2, 2001
- Destiny's Child - *Destiny Fulfilled ... And Lovin' It Farwell Tour* - July 2, 2005
- Beyoncé - *The Beyoncé Experience Tour* - July 6, 2007 & *I Am... Tour* - July 3, 2009
- Rihanna - *The Good Girl Gone Bad Tour* - July 4, 2008
- July 2-4, 2010 - The 2010 Essence Music Festival

Other Events

- September 13, 1987 – Mass (attended by an estimated 80,000) conducted by Pope John Paul II.
- 1988 – The 1988 Republican Party national convention, which nominated George H. W. Bush, of Texas, for U.S. President and Dan Quayle, of Indiana, for the Vice Presidency.
- 2005 – Hurricane Katrina evacuation
- July 22-26, 2009 – The 2009 ELCA Youth Gathering. (The Dome showcased multiple performers, speakers, and bands, many of national prominence, during the five days of the gathering.)
- July 17-21, 2010 – The 2010 LCMS National Youth Gathering

External links

- Official Louisiana Superdome website [1]
- Southeastern Architectural Archive, Tulane University [2]

Hurrican Katrina

Effect of Hurricane Katrina on the New Orleans Saints

After Hurricane Katrina devastated the city of New Orleans on August 29, 2005 and caused extensive damage to the Louisiana Superdome, the New Orleans Saints were not able to play any home games there for the entire 2005 NFL season. After practicing for approximately a week in San Jose, California, where they had evacuated in conjunction with a pre-season game against the Oakland Raiders, the team set up temporary headquarters and arranged for practice facilities in San Antonio, Texas, where owner Tom Benson started his car dealership empire. The league then announced that although the Saints' first home game on September 18 against the New York Giants would be played at Giants Stadium at 7:30 p.m. EDT on September 19, other home games would be split between Tiger Stadium at LSU in Baton Rouge, Louisiana (80 miles/130 km from New Orleans), and the Alamodome in San Antonio (540 miles/869 km from New Orleans); offices and practice would remain in San Antonio throughout the season. Various media reports in the San Antonio Express-News indicated the owner and government officials in San Antonio were working behind the scenes concerning a possible permanent relocation to San Antonio. San Antonio Mayor Phil Hardberger has pushed a strong verbal campaign to pursue the Saints. Other officials, including Texas Governor Rick Perry, had indicated they would also support a relocation to San Antonio, including using funding to upgrade the Alamodome, or possibly build a new stadium. Dallas Cowboys owner Jerry Jones, whose team currently has San Antonio as part of its territorial rights, also supported an NFL team moving to San Antonio. However, the NFL and commissioner Paul Tagliabue are in favor of keeping the franchise in New Orleans, or at least delaying a decision on a potential relocation. Other rumors say that the NFL prefers to move the team to Los Angeles, or even prefers to expand to Toronto instead, as both cities are over twice the size of San Antonio.

Many fans in Louisiana were angered and felt that Hardberger and Perry were taking advantage of New Orleans' misfortunes to try to steal the Saints. Benson's actions also drew the anger of New Orleans Mayor Ray Nagin, who called Benson's actions shameful and disrespectful to New Orleans fans who have supported the team for nearly four decades of mostly losing seasons. San Antonio officials, on the other hand, countered that Benson may have no choice—New Orleans may never fully recover as a viable location for an NFL franchise, and they are simply giving the franchise an option to relocate and remain economically viable, in this case to a city in which Benson already lives and has business interests. Benson indicated in his open letter to the Gulf Coast that San Antonio officials are only doing what any city seeking a franchise would do—recruit the franchise.

Prospective relocation controversy

On October 21, 2005, Benson issued a statement saying that he had not made any decision about the future of the Saints. However, the *San Antonio Express-News* reported that sources close to the Saints' organization said that Benson planned to void his lease agreement with New Orleans by declaring the Louisiana Superdome unusable.

NFL Commissioner Paul Tagliabue met with Benson and Louisiana governor Kathleen Blanco at the Saints' first home game in Baton Rouge on October 30 against the Miami Dolphins. After the meeting, he stopped just short of making a formal commitment to keep the Saints in New Orleans. Said Tagliabue: "The Saints are Louisiana's team and have been since the late '60s when my predecessor Pete Rozelle welcomed them to the league as New Orleans' team and Louisiana's team. Our focus continues to be on having the Saints in Louisiana." He dispelled rumors that had the Saints relocating to Los Angeles. Tagliabue appointed an eight-owner advisory committee to help decide the team's future. Benson left the game with five minutes left in the fourth quarter. A WWL-TV camera crew recorded him leaving the stadium. Benson angrily pushed the camera away and then got into an argument with a fan. Video of the altercation was obtained by WWL-TV. Three days later, Benson issued a statement that he would no longer go to Baton Rouge for Saints home games because he felt he and his family were in danger from abuse at the game.

The following day, Benson agreed with Louisiana state officials to extend his opt out clause with the Superdome and Louisiana because of the disaster until January 2007.

In the midst of the Katrina relocation controversy, several groups of investors approached Benson with offers to buy the team and keep them in Louisiana, the most notable group being one led by Fox Sports analyst and former Pittsburgh Steelers quarterback Terry Bradshaw, who is a Louisiana native. However, Benson expressed that he had no intention of selling the team and plans to eventually hand down ownership to his granddaughter, Saints owner/executive Rita Benson LeBlanc. Benson spoke to press following an NFL owners' meeting on November 15, during which he reiterated that the team is not for sale, but also stated that other NFL owners, along with Tagliabue, were working with him to keep the team in New Orleans.

On December 5, Tagliabue met with Benson and New Orleans officials to tour the city and assess the viability of playing in New Orleans in 2006. On January 11, 2006, at a press conference in New Orleans, Tagliabue announced that the Saints would likely play all eight home games at the Superdome. Superdome officials said January 12 that the Dome will be ready by September 1, 2006. The NFL announced on February 5, 2006, that the Superdome would reopen on September 24 when the Saints were to host the Atlanta Falcons.

Tagliabue said the team's preseason games would likely be played elsewhere in the region. He also stated that the Saints and the NFL were committed to New Orleans for the long haul.

Starting in the fall of 2006, the Saints returned to playing all of their regular home games of the 2006 season in New Orleans at the Superdome.

In April 2009, the franchise reached a deal that would keep the Saints in New Orleans until at least 2025.

Seasons 2006-2010

2006 New Orleans Saints season

The **2006 New Orleans Saints season** began with the team trying to improve on their 3-13 record in 2005. All of the team's 2006 regular season home games were played in the Louisiana Superdome, which had been damaged all of the previous season by Hurricane Katrina. At the time, it had been New Orleans' most successful season, with the team reaching the NFC Championship for the first time in franchise history.

Offseason

On January 17, the Saints made their first step in the 2006 offseason by hiring Sean Payton, the former assistant head coach for the Dallas Cowboys, as their new head coach.

On March 14, 2006, the Saints acquired former-Chargers QB Drew Brees through free agency, where he signed a six-year deal with them.

In the 2006 NFL Draft, the Saints used their first pick on the 2005 Heisman Trophy winner from USC, Reggie Bush, who was passed over by the Houston Texans, who instead selected North Carolina St. defensive end Mario Williams with the first overall pick. They then used their picks on Alabama Safety Roman Harper, Bloomsburg OT Jahri Evans, Purdue DE Rob Ninkovich, Oregon St. WR Mike Hass, Pittsburgh CB Josh "Bernard" Lay, Northwestern OT Zach Strief, and Hofstra WR Marques Colston.

Return to New Orleans

The NFL announced on February 5, 2006, that the Superdome would reopen on September 24 when the Saints hosted the Atlanta Falcons.

Sites for the team's 2006 preseason games were announced on March 23. They are Shreveport, Louisiana, for an August 21 game against the Dallas Cowboys, and Jackson, Mississippi, for an August 26 game against the Indianapolis Colts.

On April 6 the Saints released their 2006 schedule. All home games are scheduled to be played at the Superdome. The home opener against the Atlanta Falcons was moved from September 24 to September 25 and was shown on ESPN's Monday Night Football.

2006 Unofficial active depth chart

Offense

WR	Marques Colston 12	Devery Henderson 19	Terrance Copper 18
LT	Jammal Brown 70	Rob Petitti 79	
LG	Jamar Nesbit 67	Montrae Holland 61	
C	Jeff Faine 52	Jonathan Goodwin 76	
RG	Jahri Evans 73	Montrae Holland 61	
RT	Jon Stinchcomb 78	Zach Strief 64	
TE	Ernie Conwell 85	Mark Campbell 80	Nate Lawrie 82
WR	Joe Horn 87	Jamal Jones 89	Lance Moore 16
QB	Drew Brees 9	Jamie Martin 10	Jason Fife 11
RB	Deuce McAllister 26	Reggie Bush 25	Aaron Stecker 27
FB	Mike Karney 44	Corey McIntyre 36	

Defense

LDE	Charles Grant 94	Eric Moore 95	
NT	Hollis Thomas 99	Antwan Lake 96	Rodney Leisle 77
DT	Brian Young 66	Willie Whitehead 98	
RDE	Will Smith 91	Eric Moore 95	
SLB	Scott Fujita 55	Alfred Fincher 56	
MLB	Mark Simoneau 53	Danny Clark 54	
WLB	Scott Shanle 58	Terrence Melton 51	
LCB	Mike McKenzie 34	DeJuan Groce 28	Curtis Deloatch 39
SS	Omar Stoutmire 23	Steve Gleason 37	Jay Bellamy 20
FS	Josh Bullocks 29	Bryan Scott 24	Jay Bellamy 20
RCB	Fred Thomas 22	Jason Craft 21	

Special teams

LS	Kevin Houser 47		
P	Steve Weatherford 7		
H	Jamie Martin 10		
K	John Carney 3		
KO	Billy Cundiff		
PR	Michael Lewis 84	Reggie Bush 25	
KR	Michael Lewis 84	Terrance Copper 18	Aaron Stecker 27

2006 schedule

Preseason (1-3)

Date	Opponent	Result	Venue
August 12, 2006	Tennessee Titans	**W** 19-16	LP Field
August 21, 2006	Dallas Cowboys	**L** 30-7	Independence Stadium
August 26, 2006	Indianapolis Colts	**L** 27-14	Veterans Memorial Stadium
August 31, 2006	Kansas City Chiefs	**L** 10-9	Arrowhead Stadium

Regular season (10-6)

Week	Date	Opponent	Result	Venue
1	September 10, 2006	Cleveland Browns	**W** 19-14	Cleveland Browns Stadium
2	September 17, 2006	Green Bay Packers	**W** 34-27	Lambeau Field
3	September 25, 2006	Atlanta Falcons	**W** 23-3	Louisiana Superdome
4	October 1, 2006	Carolina Panthers	**L** 21-18	Bank of America Stadium
5	October 8, 2006	Tampa Bay Buccaneers	**W** 24-21	Louisiana Superdome

6	October 15, 2006	Philadelphia Eagles	W 27-24	Louisiana Superdome
7	Bye			
8	October 29, 2006	Baltimore Ravens	L 22-35	Louisiana Superdome
9	November 5, 2006	Tampa Bay Buccaneers	W 31-14	Raymond James Stadium
10	November 12, 2006	Pittsburgh Steelers	L 31-38	Heinz Field
11	November 19, 2006	Cincinnati Bengals	L 31-16	Louisiana Superdome
12	November 26, 2006	Atlanta Falcons	W 31-13	Georgia Dome
13	December 3, 2006	San Francisco 49ers	W 34-10	Louisiana Superdome
14	December 10, 2006	Dallas Cowboys	W 42-17	Texas Stadium
15	December 17, 2006	Washington Redskins	L 16-10	Louisiana Superdome
16	December 24, 2006	New York Giants	W 30-7	Giants Stadium
17	December 31, 2006	Carolina Panthers	L 21-31	Louisiana Superdome

Postseason (1-1)

Week	Date	Opponent	Result	Venue
Wildcard Round	Bye			
Divisional Round	January 13, 2007	Philadelphia Eagles	W 27-24	Louisiana Superdome
NFC Championship	January 21, 2007	Chicago Bears	L 39-14	Soldier Field

Regular season

Week 1: at Cleveland Browns

The Saints opened the regular season on the road against the Cleveland Browns on September 10. In the first half, kicker John Carney provided all of the Saints' first 9 points. He put up a 43-yarder in the first, along with a 25 and a 21-yarder in the second quarter. In the third quarter, the Browns offense finally got going as Cleveland QB Charlie Frye hooked up with TE Kellen Winslow on an 18-yard TD pass. Fortunately, the Saints would respond with a 12-yard TD pass from QB Drew Brees to WR

Marques Colston. In the fourth quarter, the Browns came close with Frye getting a 1-yard TD run. However, the Saints put the game away with Carney kicking a 20-yard FG to give the Saints the win.

Despite not scoring a TD, RB Reggie Bush had a sound NFL debut, as he ran 14 times for 61 yards, caught 8 passes for 58 yards, and returned three punts for 22 Yards. In total, he piled up 141 all-purpose yards.

Week 2: at Green Bay Packers

For Week 2, the Saints traveled to Lambeau Field in Green Bay, Wisconsin to take on the Packers. The Saints trailed in the first quarter, as a 22-yard TD pass to opposing WR Greg Jennings and two Dave Rayner field goals (a 24-yarder and a 36-yarder). The Saints began their scoring in the second quarter, as RB Deuce McAllister got a 3-yard TD run and QB Drew Brees threw a 26-yard TD strike to WR Devery Henderson. In the third quarter, the punishing continued, as kicker John Carney kicked a 45 and a 47-yard field goal to further New Orleans' lead. In the fourth quarter, Green Bay tried to come back with QB Brett Favre throwing a 4-yard pass to WR Robert Ferguson. The Saints managed to put the game away with a 25-yard TD pass to WR Marques Colston and a 23-yard run by McAllister. The Packers would get one more score, in the form of a 6-yard TD pass to RB Noah Herron, but the damage had already been done.

Week 3: vs. Atlanta Falcons

Riding high from their two-straight road wins, the Saints returned home to the Louisiana Superdome for the first time since December 26, 2004 for a special Monday Night game against their fellow NFC South division rival, the Atlanta Falcons, in front of a sell-out crowd of 70,003 and ESPN's largest-ever audience, with about 10.8 million households viewing, the second-largest cable audience in history (behind the 1993 North American Free Trade Agreement (NAFTA) debate between Al Gore and Ross Perot on CNN).On just the fourth overall play of the game, Safety Steve Gleason blocked a punt and DB Curtis Deloatch managed to land on the ball in the end zone for the Saints first score of the game. Former Saints kicker Morten Andersen helped Atlanta get its only score of the game, from a 26-yard field goal. From there, the Saints dominated the rest of the game. For the final score of the first quarter, WR Devery Henderson ran 11 yards for a touchdown on a reverse. Kicker John Carney would provide the scoring for the rest of the game, as he kicked two second quarter field goals (a 37-yarder and a 51-yarder), and one third quarter field goal (a 20-yarder) to essentially wrap up the game. From there, the Saints defense continued to put pressure on Falcons QB Michael Vick, as they sacked him five times, while limiting the running duo of Vick and Dunn to just a combined total of 101 rushing yards. With their dominating performance, the Saints would take the lead in the NFC South with a surprising 3-0 record.

Green Day and U2 performed jointly on the field before the game, while the Goo Goo Dolls held a concert outside the Dome earlier in the evening.

Week 4: at Carolina Panthers

Following their dominant home game at the Louisiana Superdome, the Saints traveled to Bank of America Stadium for an NFC South battle with the Carolina Panthers. From the get-go, the Saints trailed early, as QB Jake Delhomme completed a 9-yard TD pass to WR Steve Smith for the only score of the period. In the second quarter, the Saints managed to get a field goal, as kicker John Carney nailed one from 31 yards out. After a scoreless third quarter, RB Deuce McAllister managed to help New Orleans take the lead, as he got a 3-yard TD run. Unfortunately, that would be the only time in the game that the Saints saw the lead, as the Panthers slashed away, with Delhomme completing a 4-yard pass to WR Drew Carter and RB DeShaun Foster running 43 yards for a touchdown. New Orleans would try to come back, as QB Drew Brees completed an 86-yard touchdown pass to WR Marques Colston, but that would be as close as they would get, as Carolina held on to win, while the Saints got their first loss of the year dropping to 3-1.

Week 5: vs. Tampa Bay Buccaneers

The second game back in the Superdome was not marked by the media attention of the Saints' home opener, but fans in attendance were not disappointed. The sold-out crowd was treated to a dramatic contest between the Saints and the Tampa Bay Buccaneers. Though Tampa Bay proved to be a formidable opponent despite their season-long losing streak, the Saints won 24-21. The win was capped off by a fourth quarter punt return by Saints rookie Reggie Bush. Prior to the play, Bush roused the notoriously raucous New Orleans audience to their feet; by the time the ball was snapped, the cheers had reached a tremendous level. The noise only increased as Bush raced past the Bucs' special teams for 65 yards and scored the game-winning touchdown, his first as an NFL player. After the game, the traditional "Who Dat?" cheer was punctuated by spontaneous chants of "Reggie, Reggie" as the Saints claimed their fourth win of the season while improving to 4-1.

Week 6: vs. Philadelphia Eagles

Hoping to build on their win over Tampa Bay, the Saints stayed at home for a Week 6 fight with the Philadelphia Eagles. In the first quarter, New Orleans jumped out to an early lead with kicker John Carney kicking a 39-yard field goal and QB Drew Brees completing a 14-yard TD pass to WR Joe Horn. In the second quarter, Philadelphia would get on the board with kicker David Akers kicking a 47-yard field goal. Fortunately, the Saints managed to further themselves, as Brees completed a 7-yard TD pass to WR Marques Colston. However, in the third quarter, the Eagles started to get back into the game, as QB Donovan McNabb completed two touchdown passes (a 60-yarder to WR Reggie Brown and a 4-yard to TE L.J. Smith). In the fourth quarter, Philadelphia took the lead on a 15-yard TD run by Brown. Fortunately, after Brees completed a 48-yard TD pass to Horn, Carney helped give New Orleans the win as he kicked a 31-yard field goal as time ran out on the game. With the win, the Saints maintained their lead in the NFC South with a 5-1 record going into their bye week.

Week 8: vs. Baltimore Ravens

Coming off their bye week, the Saints stayed at home for their Week 8 fight with the visiting Baltimore Ravens. From the get-go, New Orleans trailed as QB Steve McNair got a 5-yard TD run for the only score of the quarter. In the second quarter, things only got worse for the Saints, as McNair completed a 4-yard TD pass to WR Clarence Moore, while rookie DB Ronnie Prude returned an interception 12 yards for a touchdown. New Orleans would get on the board, as QB Drew Brees completed a 32-yard TD pass to WR Joe Horn, yet Baltimore would increase their lead with McNair completing a 6-yard TD pass to TE Todd Heap. In the third quarter, the Ravens got another 12-yard TD interception return with rookie Strong Safety Dawan Landry making the pick for the only score of the period. In the fourth quarter, the Saints tried to mount a comeback, as Brees completed a 47-yard TD pass and a 25-yard TD pass to rookie WR Marques Colston. However, the Saints comeback drive would end there, as New Orleans fell to 5-2.

Week 9: at Tampa Bay Buccaneers

Hoping to rebound from their home loss to the Ravens, the Saints flew to Raymond James Stadium for an NFC South rematch with the Tampa Bay Buccaneers. In the first quarter, QB Drew Brees completed a 15-yard TD pass to rookie WR Marques Colston and a 52-yard TD pass to WR Devery Henderson. In the second quarter, kicker John Carney would complete a 46-yard field goal to give New Orleans a 17-0 lead. Yet, the Bucs started to fight back, as QB Bruce Gradkowski completed two touchdown passes to WR Joey Galloway (a 44-yarder and a 17-yarder). In the third quarter, the Saints would take over for the rest of the game, as RB Deuce McAllister completed a 3-yard TD run, while Brees completed a 45-yard TD pass to Henderson. After a scoreless fourth quarter, New Orleans would get the sweep over Tampa Bay and improve to 6-2.

Week 10: at Pittsburgh Steelers

Coming off their sweeping win over the Bucs, the Saints flew to Heinz Field for a match-up with the defending Super Bowl champion Pittsburgh Steelers. In the first quarter, the Saints trailed early as QB Ben Roethlisberger completed a 37-yard TD pass to WR Hines Ward and a 2-yard TD pass to TE Heath Miller. Afterwards, New Orleans got on the board with QB Drew Brees completing a 3-yard TD pass to WR Terrance Copper. In the second quarter, the Saints started to take command as kicker John Carney completed a 20-yard field goal, while rookie RB Reggie Bush got a 15-yard TD run on a reverse. Pittsburgh would get kicker Jeff Reed to get a 32-yard field goal, yet New Orleans responded with RB Deuce McAllister getting a 4-yard TD run. In the third quarter, the Steelers started to fight back as Roethlisberger completed a 38-yard TD pass to WR Cedrick Wilson for the only score of the period. In the fourth quarter, RB Willie Parker followed up two 70+ yard runs with a 3-yard and a 4-yard TD run to give Pittsburgh the lead. The Saints tried to fight back with McAllister getting a 4-yard TD run, but Pittsburgh held on to win. With the loss, the Saints fell to 6-3.

Week 11: vs. Cincinnati Bengals

Coming off a road loss to the Steelers, the Saints went home for an interconference fight with the Cincinnati Bengals. In the first quarter, Cincinnati struck first with QB Carson Palmer completing a 41-yard TD pass to WR Chad Johnson. Afterwards, New Orleans responded with QB Drew Brees completing a 72-yard TD pass to WR Joe Horn. In the second quarter, the Bengals took the lead with kicker Shayne Graham getting a 21-yard field goal for the only score of the period. After a scoreless third quarter, kicker John Carney began the fourth quarter with 24-yard field goal. However, things went downhill with Cincinnati's most dominant part of the game. Palmer would complete a 60-yard TD pass and a 4-yard TD pass to Chad, while rookie DB Ethan Kilmer returned an interception 52 yards for a touchdown. Afterwards, New Orleans could only muster a 27-yard TD pass from Brees to WR Terrance Copper. With the loss, the Saints fell to 6-4.

Week 12: at Atlanta Falcons

Trying to snap a two-game skid, the Saints flew to the Georgia Dome for an NFC South rematch with the Atlanta Falcons. In the first quarter, New Orleans started off strong with QB Drew Brees completing a 76-yard TD pass to WR Devery Henderson, while RB Deuce McAllister got a 1-yard TD run. Afterwards, Falcons kicker Morten Andersen completed a 22-yard field goal for Atlanta. In the second quarter, Andersen would give the Falcons a 30-yard field goal, while on the final play of the half, Brees threw a spectacular 48-yard "Hail Mary" TD pass to WR Terrance Copper. In the third quarter, Atlanta tried to fight back, as RB Warrick Dunn got a 1-yard TD run for the only score of the quarter. In the fourth quarter, New Orleans managed to put the game away with kicker John Carney completing a 25-yard field goal and McAllister getting a 9-yard TD run. With the season sweep over the Falcons, the Saints improved to 7-4.

Week 13: vs. San Francisco 49ers

Attempting to capitalize on their decisive victory at Atlanta, a revitalized Saints team entered the game with high hopes. In the first quarter, 49ers kicker Joe Nedney kicked a 29-yarder for the 49ers only score of the half. Reggie Bush exploded in the second quarter with a 1-yard run TD and, after an interception returned to the 7-yard line by Mike McKenzie, a sneak-around TD late in the quarter. Coming into the third quarter, Alex Smith completed a 48-yard TD pass to Antonio Bryant, but that was the final score for the 49ers. After a John Carney field goal, Reggie Bush took hold of a five-yard shovel pass from Drew Brees and scored his third TD of the night. In the fourth quarter, Bush ran down the sidelines and appeared to be heading for a fourth touchdown after a quick pass that he turned into a 74-yarder, but he fumbled the ball out of bounds. However, he scored on a ten-yard run a few plays later, and kicker John Carney sent the game away with a 33-yard field goal. With the win, the Saints improve to 8-4.

Week 14: at Dallas Cowboys

After a spectacular offensive performance all around by the Saints against the 49ers, they headed to Dallas to face off against their NFC rivals the Cowboys. The Cowboys started off strong with a 77-yard Julius Jones run, but they were silent for the rest of the quarter. In the second quarter, a shaky Saints team suddenly scored on all three of their drives: a 2-yard run from Mike Karney, a 3-yard pass from Drew Brees to Karney, and a 27-yard pass from Brees to WR Jamal Jones; and to cap it all off, Dallas kicker Martin Gramatica missed a field goal at the end of the half. A surprising Saints team stymied the Cowboys to a field goal by Gramatica, and Reggie Bush quickly answered with a 61-yard catch for a TD. Terrell Owens answered with a 34-yard touchdown catch. Mike Karney struck again with a 6-yard catch, and after a challenge by Sean Payton it was ruled a TD. The Saints recovered an onside kick at the 40, and Devery Henderson caught a 42-yard pass and crawled in for a touchdown. With the blowout against the Cowboys, the Saints improved to 9-4 and are one game away from clinching the NFC South. Mike Karney was called by Drew Brees 'Mr. Touchdown,' because he had three TD's.

Week 15: vs. Washington Redskins

The Washington Redskins entered the game strongly, with a solid drive straight down the field, but blitz, a fumble, and a penalty all worked against the Redskins, and forced a 37-yard field goal. However, they stifled the Saints offense and scored a quick TD later. The Saints answered back with a touchdown from the goal line, and limit the Redskins to a field goal. The surprising Redskins offense was hindered in the second quarter, as were the Saints, but in the beginning of the fourth, the Saints opened up with a field goal, which the Redskins quickly answered. In a key play, the Saints converted a 4th-and-5 play late in the fourth quarter, down 16-10, which led to another key 16-yard throw on third down on the 2 minute warning. Reggie Bush made a dash to the twenty-yard line two plays later, and the Saints took their second time out with 1:01 left in the 4th quarter. On 4th and 8 with 53 seconds left, Carlos Rogers knocked the ball down and sealed the Saints' fate. With the loss, the Saints fell to 9-5, but because the Carolina Panthers fell to the Pittsburgh Steelers (along with the Atlanta Falcons falling to the Dallas Cowboys), they clinched the NFC South and a spot in the playoffs.

Week 16: at New York Giants

Despite the loss the previous week, the Saints could clinch a first-round bye with a win and help. They entered the Meadowlands against a New York Giants team trying to gain momentum that could lead them to a playoff spot. Hoping they could capitalize off the Saints loss, the Giants' first drive saw a 55-yard touchdown pass from Eli Manning to Plaxico Burress. The Saints' offense opened with a three-and-out, but they successfully recovered their punt. A field goal narrowed the score to 7-3. A subsequent Saints drive ended with another field goal. With 10:30 left in the second quarter, the Saints directed a huge, time-eating drive that ended with a touchdown on fourth-down with just 1:56 left in the half. Seven minutes into the third quarter, Reggie Bush sped past the Giants' linebacker corps and scored on a one-yard TD, to lengthen the score to 20-7. In the middle of the third quarter, Reggie Bush returned a punt, fell onto his knees (but because nobody touched him he was not down by contact), and he then ran the ball in for a touchdown. However, a challenge revealed that the Giants' punter just barely nicked the leg of Bush, and he was ruled down by contact. Early in the fourth quarter, Deuce McAllister ran it in for the final TD of the day, and John Carney sealed it with a 38-yard field goal. The Saints defense was stout throughout the game, shutting out the Giants after their opening touchdown, and never allowing the Giants to run a play in their territory. With the win, the Saints improved to 10-5. The following day, the Dallas Cowboys fell to the revitalized, Jeff Garcia-led Philadelphia Eagles, and the Saints secured the #2 spot in the NFC, and a first-round bye.

Week 17: vs. Carolina Panthers

The New Orleans Saints hosted the final game in their regular season against their NFC South Rivals, the Carolina Panthers at 12:00 Central Time in the Superdome. On December 29, 2006, the Friday before the game, the Saints announced several roster moves. Players, such as RB Jamaal Branch, were activated from the practice squad. It was widely speculated that this was to help give some of the full-time starters rest before the post-season. The Saints allowed the starters to play in the first drive on offense, which ended up in a quick touchdown, and for the first two plays of the second drive, before resting all of the starters. The head coach of the Saints, Sean Payton, did this to prevent injuries before the playoff game. The Carolina Panthers ended up scraping together a meaningless victory against the second and third stringers of the Saints 31-21.

Playoffs

NFC Divisional Round: vs. Philadelphia Eagles

Being in the divisional round for only the second time in franchise history, the second-seeded Saints began their playoff run against the third-seeded Philadelphia Eagles. With both teams coming into the game with the NFL's best offenses, the outlook was a high-scoring shootout. In the first quarter, New Orleans drew first blood with kicker John Carney nailing a 33-yard field goal for the only score of the period. In the second quarter, the Saints increased its lead with Carney kicking a 23-yard field goal. However, the Eagles took the lead with QB Jeff Garcia completing a 75-yard TD pass to former Saints wide receiver Donte' Stallworth. New Orleans retook the lead with rookie RB Reggie Bush ramming a 4-yard TD run; yet Philadelphia regained the lead with RB Brian Westbrook diving for a 1-yard TD run to exit the second quarter with a 14-13 lead. In the third quarter, the Eagles jabbed at the Saints' once-stoic running defense with another Westbrook TD run, this one for 62 yards. The Saints countered with RB Deuce McAllister shoving his way in with a 5-yard TD run; and finally, the Saints scored their final touchdown for the lead with a knockout 11-yard TD pass from Drew Brees to McAllister. In the fourth quarter, the Eagles drove down to the red zone and threatened to strike, but the Saints' defense stepped up and forced kicker David Akers to kick his only score for the Eagles, a 24 yard field goal. Suddenly it looked grim for the Saints when, on the ensuing drive, a pitch-out from Brees to Bush bounced off the running back's hands and the Eagles recovered. However, the Saints defense forced a 4th-and-10, and an 18-yard pass that seemed keep the Eagles alive was called back on a false start penalty. The Eagles punted with 1:39 remaining, and the Saints converted a first down to end the game.

During the game, the Saints made a franchise playoff record with 435 total yards of offense. Deuce McAllister gained a franchise playoff record 143 yards on 21 carries with 1 touchdown, along with 4 catches for 20 yards and 1 touchdown.

With the win, New Orleans improved its overall record to 11-6 and advanced to its first NFC Championship Game appearance in the team's 40-year franchise history, where they took on the Chicago Bears.

NFC Championship Game: at Chicago Bears

Following their divisional win over the Eagles, the Saints flew to Soldier Field for their very first NFC Championship Game, where they would take on the top-seeded Chicago Bears. In the first quarter, New Orleans trailed early with Bears kicker Robbie Gould getting a 19-yard field goal for the only score of the period. In the second quarter, the Saints continued to trail as Gould gave Chicago a 43-yard and a 23-yard field goal, while RB Thomas Jones got a 2-yard TD run. New Orleans would manage to get some momentum for the second half as QB Drew Brees completed a 13-yard TD pass to rookie WR Marques Colston. In the third quarter, the Saints started to get more momentum as Brees completed an 88-yard TD pass to rookie RB Reggie Bush. However, the Bears began to creep back, getting a safety when Brees was called for intentional grounding while in his own endzone. In the fourth quarter, New Orleans' struggles continued with Chicago QB Rex Grossman completing a 33-yard TD pass to WR Bernard Berrian. Also, Bears RB Cedric Benson got a 12-yard TD run, while Jones wrapped up the game with a 15-yard TD run.

A key factor to New Orleans' loss was the fact that they were a "dome" team and were forced to play in snowy conditions while committing five turnovers (three lost fumbles, an interception, and one on downs).

With the loss, the Saints season ended with an overall record of 11-7.

2007 New Orleans Saints season

The **2007 New Orleans Saints season** was the 41st season for the team in the National Football League. The team tried to improve upon its 10-6 record in 2006 and its third division title—the Saints' first in the NFC South. Their other two division titles were in the NFC West, prior to the league's 2002 realignment. After opening up the pre-season in the Hall of Fame Game against the Pittsburgh Steelers on August 5, 2007, the Saints ended with a 3-2 pre-season record. The Saints opened the regular season with a nationally televised game against the defending Super Bowl champion Indianapolis Colts, but ultimately had a disappointing season, finishing 2007 with a 7-9 record and missing out on post-season play.

Coaching staff

Head coach Sean Payton was entering his second year with the Saints. He was joined with offensive coordinator Doug Marrone and defensive coordinator Gary Gibbs.

Schedule

Preseason

Week	Date	Opponent	Time	Game Site	TV	Result/Score	Record
HF	August 5, 2007	Pittsburgh Steelers	8:00 pm EDT	Fawcett Stadium	NFL Network	L 20-7	0-1
1	August 10, 2007	Buffalo Bills	8:00 pm EDT	Louisiana Superdome	CBS	L 13-10	0-2
2	August 18, 2007	Cincinnati Bengals	7:30 pm EDT	Paul Brown Stadium	CST	W 27-19	1-2
3	August 23, 2007	Kansas City Chiefs	8:30 pm EDT	Arrowhead Stadium	CST	W 30-7	2-2
4	August 30, 2007	Miami Dolphins	8:00 pm EDT	Louisiana Superdome	CST	W 7-0	3-2

HF = Hall of Fame Game

Regular season

Week	Date	Opponent	Time	Game Site	TV	Result/Score	Record
1	September 6, 2007	Indianapolis Colts	8:30 pm EDT	RCA Dome	NBC	L 41 - 10	0 - 1
2	September 16, 2007	Tampa Bay Buccaneers	1:00 pm EDT	Raymond James Stadium	Fox	L 31 - 14	0 - 2
3	September 24, 2007	Tennessee Titans	8:30 pm EDT	Louisiana Superdome	ESPN	L 31 - 14	0 - 3
4	Bye						
5	October 7, 2007	Carolina Panthers	1:00 pm EDT	Louisiana Superdome	Fox	L 16 - 13	0 - 4
6	October 14, 2007	Seattle Seahawks	8:15 pm EDT	Qwest Field	NBC	W 28 - 17	1 - 4
7	October 21, 2007	Atlanta Falcons	1:00 pm EDT	Louisiana Superdome	Fox	W 22 - 16	2 - 4
8	October 28, 2007	San Francisco 49ers	4:15 pm EDT	Monster Park	Fox	W 31 - 10	3 - 4
9	November 4, 2007	Jacksonville Jaguars	1:00 pm EST	Louisiana Superdome	CBS	W 41 - 24	4 - 4
10	November 11, 2007	St. Louis Rams	1:00 pm EST	Louisiana Superdome	Fox	L 37 - 29	4 - 5
11	November 18, 2007	Houston Texans	1:00 pm EST	Reliant Stadium	Fox	L 23 - 10	4 - 6
12	November 25, 2007	Carolina Panthers	1:00 pm EST	Bank of America Stadium	Fox	W 31 - 6	5 - 6
13	December 2, 2007	Tampa Bay Buccaneers	1:00 pm EST	Louisiana Superdome	Fox	L 27 - 23	5 - 7
14	December 10, 2007	Atlanta Falcons	8:30 pm EST	Georgia Dome	ESPN	W 34 - 14	6 - 7
15	December 16, 2007	Arizona Cardinals	1:00 pm EST	Louisiana Superdome	Fox	W 31-24	7 - 7
16	December 23, 2007	Philadelphia Eagles	1:00 pm EST	Louisiana Superdome	Fox	L 38-23	7 - 8
17	December 30, 2007	Chicago Bears	1:00 pm EST	Soldier Field	Fox	L 33-25	7-9

Week-by-week results

Week 1: at Indianapolis Colts

Game summary

The 2007 New Orleans Saints began their regular season in the annual Thursday night Kickoff game against the defending Super Bowl champion Indianapolis Colts. In the first quarter, New Orleans trailed early as Super Bowl XLI MVP Peyton Manning completed a 27-yard TD pass to WR Marvin Harrison for the score of the period. In the second quarter, the Saints managed to get their only touchdown of the game as DB Jason David (a former Colt) returned a fumble 55 yards to the endzone. Afterwards, New Orleans took the lead with kicker Olindo Mare getting a 34-yard field goal. Indianapolis would tie the game prior to halftime with kicker Adam Vinatieri nailing a 33-yard field goal. In the second half, the Colts dominated the rest of the game. During the third quarter, RB Joseph Addai got a 2-yard TD run, while Manning hooked up with WR Reggie Wayne on a 29-yard TD pass.

For the fourth quarter, Indianapolis wrapped up the game with Vinatieri getting a 33-yard field goal, Manning & Wayne hooking up with each other again on a 45-yard TD pass, and DB Matt Giordano returning an interception 83 yards for a touchdown.

With the loss, the Saints began the year at 0-1.

Scoring summary

Q1 - IND - 1:36 - 27 yard TD pass from Peyton Manning to Marvin Harrison (Adam Vinatieri kick) (IND 7-0)

Q2 - NO - 11:32 - Jason David 55 yard fumble return TD (Olindo Mare kick) (7-7)

Q2 - NO - 6:30 - Olindo Mare 34 yard FG (NO 10-7)

Q2 - IND - 0:45 - Adam Vinatieri 33 yard FG (10-10)

Q3 - IND - 9:45 - Joseph Addai 2 yard TD run (Vinatieri kick) (IND 17-10)

Q3 - IND - 6:11 - 29 yard TD pass from Peyton Manning to Reggie Wayne (Vinatieri kick) (IND 24-10)

Q4 - IND - 14:12 - Adam Vinatieri 33 yard FG (IND 27-10)

Q4 - IND - 10:05 - 45yard TD pass from Peyton Manning to Reggie Wayne (Vinatieri kick) (IND 34-10)

Q4 - IND - 0:55 - Matt Giordano 83 yard interception return TD (Vinatieri kick) (IND 41-10)

Week 2: at Tampa Bay Buccaneers

Game summary

Following their season-opening loss to the Colts, the Saints flew to Raymond James Stadium for an NFC South duel with the Tampa Bay Buccaneers. In the first quarter, New Orleans trailed early as Bucs RB Carnell "Cadillac" Williams got a 1-yard TD run for the only score of the period. In the second quarter, the Saints continued to struggle as Tampa Bay QB Jeff Garcia hooked up with WR Joey Galloway on a 69-yard TD pass and a 24-yard pass.

In the third quarter, the Buccaneers extended their lead with Williams getting another 1-yard TD run. Afterwards, New Orleans finally got on the board with FB Mike Karney getting a 1-yard TD run. However, in the fourth quarter, Tampa Bay closed out the game with kicker Matt Bryant's 27-yard field goal. The Saints would get the final score of the game as QB Drew Brees completed a 4-yard TD pass to WR Marques Colston.

With the loss, the Saints fell to 0-2.

Scoring summary				
Q	Team	Time	Scoring play	Score
1	TB	5:30	Williams 1-yard TD run (Bryant kick)	TB 7-0
2	TB	13:23	69-yard TD pass from Garcia to Galloway (Bryant kick)	TB 14-0
2	TB	1:12	24-yard TD pass from Garcia to Galloway (Bryant kick)	TB 21-0
3	TB	4:32	Williams 1-yard TD run (Bryant kick)	TB 28-0
3	NO	5:55	Karney 1-yard TD run (Mare kick)	TB 28-7
4	TB	7:35	Bryant 27-yard FG	TB 31-7
4	NO	2:56	4-yard TD pass from Brees to Colston (Mare kick)	**TB 31-14**

Week 3: vs. Tennessee Titans

Trying to snap a two-game skid, the Saints played their Week 3 Monday night homeopener, as they played an interconference duel with the Tennessee Titans. In the first quarter, New Orleans' struggles continued as Titans kicker Rob Bironas nailed a 33-yard field goal, while QB Vince Young completed a 35-yard TD pass to WR Brandon Jones. In the second quarter, the Saints managed to get the only score of the period as RB Reggie Bush got a 1-yard TD run. In the third quarter, New Orleans took the lead with Bush getting another 1-yard TD run. However, Tennessee regained the lead with RB LenDale White's 1-yard TD run. In the fourth quarter, the Titans took over as Young completed a 3-yard TD pass to TE Bo Scaife, while DB Vincent Fuller ended the game with an interception return of 61 yards for a touchdown. In the game, QB Drew Brees was 29 of 45 for 225 yards with 4 interceptions (3 of them coming from LB Keith Bulluck).

With the loss, the Saints entered their Bye Week at 0-3.

Scoring summary				
Q	Team	Time	Scoring play	Score
1	TEN	2:44	Bironas 33-yard FG	TEN 3-0
2	TEN	12:55	Jones 35-yard TD pass from Young (Bironas kick)	TEN 10-0
2	NO	1:00	Bush 1-yard TD run (Mare kick)	TEN 10-7
3	NO	7:55	Bush 1-yard TD run (Mare kick)	NO 14-10
3	TEN	2:19	White 1-yard TD run (Bironas kick)	TEN 17-14
4	TEN	8:55	Scaife 3-yard TD pass from Young (Bironas kick)	TEN 24-14
4	TEN	2:39	Fuller 61-yard interception return TD (Bironas kick)	**TEN 31-14**

Week 5: vs. Carolina Panthers

Game summary

Coming off their bye week and still in search of their first win of the year, the Saints stayed at home at played a Week 5 divisional duel with the Carolina Panthers. In the first quarter, New Orleans trailed early as Panthers kicker John Kasay got a 23-yard field goal. The Saints would respond with kicker Olindo Mare getting a 25-yard field goal. In the second quarter, the Panthers retook the lead with Kasay's 35-yard field goal. New Orleans would respond with Mare kicking a 28-yard field goal.

In the third quarter, the Saints took the lead with FB Mike Karney getting a 2-yard TD run for the only score of the period. However, in the fourth quarter, Carolina came back to win with QB David Carr completing a 17-yard TD pass to WR Steve Smith, along with Kasay's 52-yard field goal as time ran out.

With the loss, the Saints fell to their first 0-4 start since 1996.

Week 6: at Seattle Seahawks

Scoring summary:

Q1 - NO - 12:38 - Pierre Thomas 5 yard fumble return (Olindo Mare kick) [NO 7-0 SEA]

Q2 - NO - 14:28 - Eric Johnson 3 yard pass from Drew Brees (Olindo Mare kick) (13-86, 7:04) [NO 14-0 SEA]

Q2 - NO - 5:18 - Lance Moore 7 yard run (Olindo Mare kick) (6-66, 2:48) [NO 21-0 SEA]

Q2 - SEA - 2:16 - Ben Obomanu 17 yard pass from Matt Hasselbeck (Josh Brown kick) (7-63 3:02) [NO 21-7 SEA]

Q2 - NO - 0:30 - Marques Colston 2 yard pass from Drew Brees (Olindo Mare kick) (9-80 1:46) [NO 28-7 SEA]

Q2 - SEA - 0:02 - Josh Brown 52 yard FG (4-38 0:28) [NO 28-10 SEA]

Q4 - SEA - 6:39 - Nate Burleson 22 yard pass from Matt Hasselbeck (Josh Brown kick) (6-80 1:31) [NO 28-17 SEA]

Week 7: vs. Atlanta Falcons

Coming off of their road win over the Seahawks, the Saints went home for a Week 7 divisional duel with the Atlanta Falcons. In the first quarter, New Orleans drew first blood as QB Drew Brees completed a 37-yard TD pass to WR Devery Henderson. The Falcons would reply with former Saints kicker Morten Andersen getting a 38-yard field goal. In the second quarter, Atlanta took lead with Andersen kicking a 33-yard field goal, along with QB Byron Leftwich completing a 9-yard TD pass to

WR Roddy White.

In the third quarter, New Orleans regained the lead with rookie RB Pierre Thomas getting a 24-yard TD run for the only score of the period. In the fourth quarter, the Falcons tried to rally as Andersen kicked a 21-yard field goal. Fortunately, the Saints sealed the win with Brees completing a 4-yard TD pass to RB Reggie Bush, with Bush getting the 2-point conversion on the ground.

With the win, New Orleans improved to 2-4.

Week 8: at San Francisco 49ers

Coming off their divisional home win over the Falcons, the Saints flew to Monster Park for a Week 8 intraconference duel with the San Francisco 49ers. In the first quarter, New Orleans drew first blood with QB Drew Brees completing a 17-yard TD pass to WR Marques Colston, along with kicker Olindo Mare getting a 26-yard field goal. In the second quarter, the Saints continued their offensive revival with Brees completing a 2-yard TD pass to WR Terrance Copper, along with a 3-yard TD pass to Colston.

In the third quarter, the 49ers tried to comeback as kicker Joe Nedney nailed a 29-yard field goal. In the fourth quarter, New Orleans managed to put the game out of reach with Brees and Colston hooking up with each other one last time on a 15-yard TD pass. Afterwards, San Francisco's only response would by QB Alex Smith completing a 7-yard TD pass to TE Vernon Davis.

With the win, the Saints improved to 3-4.

Week 9: vs. Jacksonville Jaguars

Coming off their road win over the 49ers, the Saints went home for a Week 9 interconference duel with the Jacksonville Jaguars. In the first quarter, New Orleans drew first blood as kicker Olindo Mare managed to get a 46-yard field goal, while RB Reggie Bush got a 1-yard TD run. The Jaguars would respond with QB Quinn Gray completing an 80-yard TD pass to WR Reggie Williams, along with former Saints kicker John Carney getting a 30-yard field goal. New Orleans would respond with QB Drew Brees completing a 2-yard TD pass to Bush. However, Jacksonville immediately answered as RB Maurice Jones-Drew returned a kickoff 100 yards for a touchdown to end the period. In the second quarter, the Saints regained the lead as Brees completed an 8-yard TD pass to WR Lance Moore for the only score of the period.

In the third quarter, New Orleans increased its lead with CB Mike McKenzie returning an interception 75 yards for a touchdown, while Brees completed a 4-yard TD pass to WR David Patten. In the fourth quarter, the Jaguars tried to comeback as Gray completed a 15-yard TD pass to WR Dennis Northcutt. Fortunately, the Saints closed out the game with Mare nailing a 34-yard field goal.

With the win, New Orleans improved to 4-4.

Week 10: vs. St. Louis Rams

Coming off a 41-24 victory over the Jaguars, the Saints stayed home to face the winless St. Louis Rams. The Saints started the game with an impressive opening drive that culminated in a 7-yard burst by Reggie Bush to give the Saints an early 7-0 lead. However, Rams running back Stephen Jackson answered with a 1-yard run of his own to tie the game toward the end of the 1st quarter.

Midway through the 2nd quarter, tight end Randy McMichael gave the Rams a 14-7 lead on a 2-yard pass from Jackson. Jeff Wilkins made it a two-score game with a 49-yard field goal three minutes later. The Saints went to the locker room trailing 17-7.

In the 2nd half, Wilkins kicked his 2nd field goal of the game, a 21-yard attempt, to increase the lead to 13. Toward the end of the 3rd, Isaac Bruce caught a 9-yard pass by Marc Bulger to make it a 27-7 lead, putting the Saints in danger of losing their first game since early October.

Drew Bennett added to the St. Louis lead by catching a three yard pass by Bulger to give Bulger his second touchdown of the game, and to give St. Louis a surprising 34-7 lead. Drew Brees and Billy Miller hooked up for a 1-yard pass with 11:36 left to cut the lead to 34-13. The Saints then converted a two-point conversion on a Bush run, to make it 34-15. Aaron Stecker then scored on a two-yard run with 4:42 remaining to cut it to 34-21. This time, however, they failed on the two-point conversion. With 1:55 left, a Wilkins field goal made it 37-21. The Saints scored another touchdown with 37 seconds left, but their attempt to recover the ball from an onside kick failed, and the Rams held on to defeat the Saints 37-29, giving the Rams their first victory in 2007 and dropping the Saints to 4-5.

Week 11: at Houston Texans

Hoping to rebound from their loss to the Rams, the Saints flew to Reliant Stadium for a Week 11 interconference showdown with the Houston Texans. In the first quarter, New Orleans got the early lead as kicker Olindo Mare managed to get a 52-yard field goal. However, the Texans took the lead with QB Matt Schaub completing a 73-yard TD pass to WR Andre Johnson. In the second quarter, the Saints regained the lead with QB Drew Brees completing a 6-yard TD pass to WR Devery Henderson. However, Houston retook the lead with Schaub completing a 10-yard TD pass to TE Joel Dreessen. After a scoreless third quarter, the Texans sealed the win as kicker Kris Brown nailed a 36-yarder, a 53-yarder, and a 23-yard field goal.

With the loss, New Orleans fell to 4-6. So far, all 6 of their losses came when they committed at least 2 turnovers in a game.

Week 12: at Carolina Panthers

Trying to snap a two-game losing skid, the Saints flew to Bank of America Stadium for a Week 12 NFC South rematch against the Carolina Panthers with second place on the line.

In the first quarter, New Orleans trailed early as Panthers kicker John Kasay managed to get a 45-yard field goal for the only score of the period. In the second quarter, the Saints took the lead with QB Drew Brees completing a 1-yard TD pass to TE Lance Moore, along with kicker Olindo Mare kicking a 46-yard field goal. Carolina ended the half as Kasay nailing a 29-yard field goal.

In the third quarter, New Orleans ran away with the game as Brees completed a 1-yard TD pass to WR Billy Miller, got an 8-yard TD run, and completed a 4-yard TD pass to WR Marques Colston.

With the win, the Saints improved to 5-6.

For Marques Colston, this marked his fifth-straight game of having at least 65 reception yards in one game.

Week 13: vs. Tampa Bay Buccaneers

Coming off their divisional road win over the Panthers, the Saints went home for a Week 13 NFC South rematch with the Tampa Bay Buccaneers. In the first quarter, New Orleans trailed early with Buccaneers kicker Matt Bryant getting a 27-yard field goal. Afterwards, the Saints took the lead with QB Drew Brees completing a 4-yard TD pass to WR Terrance Copper. In the second quarter, Tampa Bay regained the lead with QB Luke McCown completing a 1-yard TD pass to TE Anthony Becht, along with Bryant nailing a 31-yard field goal. Afterwards, New Orleans retook the lead with Brees completing a 45-yard TD pass to WR Devery Henderson.

In the third quarter, the Buccaneers regained the lead with RB Earnest Graham getting a 25-yard TD run. Later, the Saints retook the lead with CB Mike McKenzie returning an interception 53 yards for a touchdown. In the fourth quarter, New Orleans increased its lead with DE Will Smith taking McCown down in his endzone for a safety. However, an attempted double reverse resulted in a lost fumble. It would allow Tampa Bay to get into position for the win, as McCown completed a 4-yard TD pass to TE Jerramy Stevens.

With the heart-breaking loss, the Saints fell to 5-7.

Week 14: at Atlanta Falcons

Hoping to rebound from their divisional home loss to the Buccaneers, the Saints flew to the Georgia Dome for a Week 14 Monday Night NFC South rematch with the Atlanta Falcons. In the first quarter, New Orleans drew first blood as QB Drew Brees completed a 25-yard TD pass to WR David Patten. The Falcons would respond with QB Chris Redman completing a 33-yard TD pass to WR Roddy White. In the second quarter, the Saints started to pull away as kicker Olindo Mare managed to get a 23-yard field goal, while Brees completed a 15-yard TD pass to WR Marques Colston.

In the third quarter, New Orleans pulled away as Brees hooked up with Colston again on a 2-yard TD pass, while Safety Roman Harper returned an interception 31 yards for a touchdown. In the fourth quarter, Atlanta would get their last strike of the game as Redman completed a 13-yard TD pass to WR Michael Jenkins. The Saints would wrap up their victory with Mare nailing a 36-yard field goal.

With their second-straight season-sweeping win over the Falcons, New Orleans improved to 6-7.

Week 15: vs. Arizona Cardinals

Coming off their Monday night divisional road win over the Falcons, the Saints went home for a Week 15 intraconference duel with the Arizona Cardinals. In the first quarter, New Orleans trialed early as Cardinals QB Kurt Warner completed a 1-yard TD pass to TE Troy Bienemann. The Saints would respond with QB Drew Brees completing a 19-yard TD pass to WR Marques Colston. In the second quarter, New Orleans took the lead with RB Aaron Stecker getting a 1-yard TD run. Arizona would tie the game with Warner completing an 18-yard TD pass to WR Larry Fitzgerald, yet the Saints regained the lead prior to halftime with Brees completing a 32-yard TD pass to WR David Patten.

In the third quarter, New Orleans increased its lead with Stecker getting a 6-yard TD run. The Cardinals responded with Warner completing a 3-yard TD pass to TE Ben Patrick. The Saints would reply with kicker Martín Gramática getting a 31-yard field goal. In the fourth quarter, Arizona tried to rally as kicker Neil Rackers nailed a 26-yard field goal. Fortunately, New Orleans' defense held on for the victory.

With the win, the Saints improved to 7-7.

For Drew Brees, he's thrown 10 touchdowns and only 1 interception in the past four games.

2008 New Orleans Saints season

The **2008 New Orleans Saints season** is the 42nd season for the team in the National Football League (NFL). The Saints entered the season in an attempt improve their 7-9 record from the 2007 season.

2008 schedule

Pre-season

Week	Date	Opponent	Time	Game Site	TV	Result/Score	Record	Match Report
1	August 7, 2008	Arizona Cardinals	7:00 pm CDT	University of Phoenix Stadium	ESPN	24-10	1-0	Recap [1]
2	August 16, 2008	Houston Texans	7:00 pm CDT	Louisiana Superdome	CST	27-31	1-1	Recap [2]
3	August 23, 2008	Cincinnati Bengals	6:30 pm CDT	Paul Brown Stadium	CST	13-0	2-1	Recap [3]
4	August 28, 2008	Miami Dolphins	7:00 pm CDT	Louisiana Superdome	CST	10-14	2-2	Recap [4]

Regular season

Week	Date	Opponent	Time	Game Site	TV	Result/Score	Record	Match Report
1	September 7, 2008	Tampa Bay Buccaneers	12:00pm CDT	Louisiana Superdome	Fox	W 24-20	1-0	Recap [5]
2	September 14, 2008	Washington Redskins	12:00pm CDT	Fedex Field	Fox	L 24-29	1-1	Recap [6]
3	September 21, 2008	Denver Broncos	3:05pm CDT	Invesco Field	Fox	L 32-34	1-2	Recap [7]
4	September 28, 2008	San Francisco 49ers	12:00pm CDT	Louisiana Superdome	Fox	W 31-17	2-2	Recap [8]
5	October 6, 2008	Minnesota Vikings	7:30pm CDT	Louisiana Superdome	ESPN	L 27-30	2-3	Recap [9]
6	October 12, 2008	Oakland Raiders	12:00pm CDT	Louisiana Superdome	CBS	W 34-3	3-3	Recap [10]

7	October 19, 2008	Carolina Panthers	12:00pm CDT	Bank of America Stadium	Fox	L 7-30	3-4	Recap [11]
8	October 26, 2008	San Diego Chargers	12:00pm CDT	Wembley Stadium, London*	CBS / BBC (UK)	W 37-32	4-4	Recap [12]
9	November 2, 2008	Bye week						
10	November 9, 2008	Atlanta Falcons	12:00pm CST	Georgia Dome	Fox	L 20-34	4-5	Recap [13]
11	November 16, 2008	Kansas City Chiefs	12:00pm CST	Arrowhead Stadium	Fox	W 30-20	5-5	Recap [14]
12	November 24, 2008	Green Bay Packers	7:30pm CST	Louisiana Superdome	ESPN	W 51-29	6-5	Recap [15]
13	November 30, 2008	Tampa Bay Buccaneers	12:00pm CST	Raymond James Stadium	Fox	L 23-20	6-6	Recap [16]
14	December 7, 2008	Atlanta Falcons	12:00pm CST	Louisiana Superdome	Fox	W 29-25	7-6	Recap [17]
15	December 11, 2008	Chicago Bears	7:15pm CST	Soldier Field	NFL Network	L 27-24	7-7	Recap [18]
16	December 21, 2008	Detroit Lions	12:00pm CST	Ford Field	Fox	W 42-7	8-7	Recap [19]
17	December 28, 2008	Carolina Panthers	12:00pm CST	Louisiana Superdome	Fox	L 31-33	8-8	Recap [20]

* New Orleans was the designated home team for the game in London.

Week 1: vs. Tampa Bay Buccaneers

The Saints began their 2008 campaign at home against their NFC South foe, the Tampa Bay Buccaneers. In the first quarter, New Orleans drew first blood as QB Drew Brees completed a 39-yard TD pass to WR David Patten. The Buccaneers would reply with CB Phillip Buchanon returning an interception 26 yards for a touchdown. In the second quarter, Tampa Bay took the lead with kicker Matt Bryant getting a 37-yard field goal. In the third quarter, the Saints responded with kicker Martín Gramática getting a 34-yard field goal. The Buccaneers would answer with Bryant nailing a 33-yard field goal, yet New Orleans regained the lead with Brees completing an 84-yard TD pass to WR Devery Henderson. In the fourth quarter, Tampa Bay jumped ahead again as QB Jeff Garcia completed a 2-yard TD pass to WR Ike Hilliard. Fortunately, the Bayou faithful got the last laugh as Brees completed the game-winning 42-yard TD pass to RB Reggie Bush. Bush's girlfriend Kim Kardashian would later state in a 2009 episode of *Keeping Up with the Kardashians* ("Distance Makes the Heart Grow Fonder", aired 3 May 2009.) that she and her sister Kourtney attended the game. Kardashian and

Bush later celebrated their victory at Morton's Steakhouse.

With the win, the Saints began their season at 1-0.

Week 2: at Washington Redskins

Coming off their divisional home win over the Buccaneers, the Saints flew to FedEx Field for a Week 2 duel with the Washington Redskins. In the first quarter, New Orleans trailed early as Redskins kicker Shaun Suisham got a 22-yard field goal. In the second quarter, Washington increased its lead with Suisham's 36-yard field goal. Afterwards, the Saints took the lead with RB Pierre Thomas getting a 1-yard TD run and kicker Martín Gramática nailing a 49-yard field goal. In the third quarter, New Orleans increased its lead with QB Drew Brees completing a 19-yard TD pass to WR Robert Meachem. The Redskins started to fight back as RB Clinton Portis got a 9-yard TD run (with a failed 2-point conversion). New Orleans would respond with RB Reggie Bush returning a punt 55 yards for a touchdown. However, Washington rallied with Portis' 8-yard TD run and QB Jason Campbell's 67-yard TD pass to WR Santana Moss.

With the surprising loss, the Saints fell to 1-1.

Week 3: at Denver Broncos

Hoping to rebound from their road loss to the Redskins, the Saints flew to Invesco Field at Mile High for a Week 3 interconference duel with the Denver Broncos. In the first quarter, New Orleans trailed early as Broncos QB Jay Cutler completed a 1-yard TD pass to TE Nate Jackson. The Saints answered with kicker Martín Gramática getting a 43-yard field goal. Denver replied with Cutler completing a 35-yard TD pass to WR Brandon Marshall. In the second quarter, New Orleans continued to struggle as Broncos LB Nate Webster returned a fumble 34 yards for a touchdown. The Saints started to rally as RB Pierre Thomas got a 5-yard TD run, while RB Reggie Bush got a 23-yard TD run. Denver answered with kicker Matt Prater getting a 27-yard field goal. New Orleans closed out the half with DE Charles Grant tackling RB Andre Hall in his endzone for a safety.

In the third quarter, the Broncos replied with RB Michael Pittman getting a 2-yard TD run. The Saints answered with QB Drew Brees completing a 6-yard TD pass to Bush, yet Denver responded with Prater nailing a 34-yard field goal. In the fourth quarter, New Orleans tried to rally as Thomas got a 10-yard TD run (with a failed 2-point conversion). They even recovered a fumble and got into field goal position. However, Gramática's 43-yard attempt went wide right, ending any hope of a comeback.

With yet-another last-moment loss, the Saints fell to 1-2.

Week 4: vs. San Francisco 49ers

Trying to snap a two-game losing streak, the Saints went home for a Week 4 duel with the San Francisco 49ers. In the first quarter, New Orleans trailed early as 49ers kicker Joe Nedney got a 47-yard field goal. In the second quarter, the Saints responded with QB Drew Brees completing a 5-yard and a 33-yard TD pass to WR Lance Moore. San Francisco tried to catch up as Nedney kicked a 49-yard field goal, yet New Orleans continued its dominance as Brees completed a 47-yard TD pass to WR Robert Meachem.

In the third quarter, the 49ers tried to rally as Nedney got a 38-yard field goal. In the fourth quarter, the Saints continued its victory march as RB Deuce McAllister got a 1-yard TD run. San Francisco tried to comeback as QB J.T. O'Sullivan completed a 5-yard TD pass to WR Isaac Bruce, yet New Orleans sealed the deal with kicker Martín Gramática nailing a 31-yard field goal.

With the win, the Saints improved to 2-2.

Week 5: vs. Minnesota Vikings

Coming off their home win over the 49ers, the Saints stayed at home for a Week 5 Monday Night duel with the Minnesota Vikings. In the first quarter, New Orleans was first out of the gate as QB Drew Brees completed a 17-yard TD pass to WR Devery Henderson. The Vikings responded with CB Antoine Winfield returning a blocked field goal 59 yards for a touchdown. The Saints answered with kicker Martín Gramática getting a 35-yard field goal. Minnesota would reply with kicker Ryan Longwell getting a 53-yard field goal. In the second quarter, the Vikings took the lead as RB Chester Taylor completed a 4-yard TD pass to TE Visanthe Shiancoe, along with Longwell kicking a 33-yard field goal.

In the third quarter, New Orleans began to rally as RB Reggie Bush returned a punt 71 yards for a touchdown. In the fourth quarter, the Saints took the lead with Gramática making a 53-yard field goal and Bush returning a punt 64 yards for a touchdown. However, Minnesota rallied with QB Gus Frerotte completing a 33-yard TD pass to WR Bernard Berrian, along with Longwell nailing the game-winning 30-yard field goal.

With the heart-breaking loss, the Saints fell to 2-3.

This game was the first time in NFL history that a game had a combination of a blocked field goal, a TD pass by a non-quarterback, two field goals of 50+ yards, and two punts returned for touchdowns.

Week 6: vs. Oakland Raiders

Hoping to rebound from their MNF home loss to the Vikings, the Saints stayed at home for a Week 6 interconference duel with the Oakland Raiders. In the first quarter, New Orleans trailed early as Raiders Sebastian Janikowski got a 24-yard field goal. In the second quarter, the Saints took the lead as RB Reggie Bush got a 3-yard TD run, along with kicker Taylor Mehlhaff (recently signed due to

Martín Gramática out for the year) getting a 44-yard field goal.

In the third quarter, New Orleans added on to their lead as QB Drew Brees completed an 8-yard TD pass to RB Aaron Stecker and a 15-yard TD pass to Bush. In the fourth quarter, the Saints closed out the game with Mehlhaff nailing a 33-yard field goal and Brees completing a 2-yard TD pass to TE Mark Campbell.

With the win, New Orleans improved to 3-3.

With a 21-yard reception in the first quarter, Reggie Bush (14 att/27 yds, 3 rec/40 yards and 2 TDs), collected his 200th reception in his NFL career over the span of just 34 games, tying Anquan Boldin for the NFL record fewest games needed to do so.

Week 7: at Carolina Panthers

Coming off their dominating home win over the Raiders, the Saints began their road trip at the Bank of America Stadium for a Week 7 NFC South duel with the Carolina Panthers. In the first quarter, New Orleans trailed early as Panthers kicker John Kasay got a 39-yard field goal. In the second quarter, the Saints responded with FB Mike Karney getting a 1-yard TD run. However, Carolina answered with RB Jonathan Stewart getting an 18-yard TD run.

In the third quarter, the Panthers added on to their lead as QB Jake Delhomme completed a 39-yard TD pass to WR Steve Smith and a 4-yard TD pass to WR DeAngelo Williams. In the fourth quarter, Carolina closed out the game with Kasay nailing a 28-yard field goal.

With the embarrassing loss, New Orleans fell to 3-4.

Week 8: vs. San Diego Chargers

Hoping to rebound from their road loss to the Panthers, the Saints flew to Wembley Stadium for the 2008 International Series game with quarterback Drew Brees' former team, the San Diego Chargers. For the game, New Orleans was registered as the home team.

In the first quarter, the Saints drew first blood as rookie kicker Taylor Mehlhaff got a 23-yard field goal. The Chargers responded with kicker Nate Kaeding getting a 33-yard field goal. In the second quarter, New Orleans got a huge lead as Brees completed a 12-yard TD pass to WR Devery Henderson (with a failed PAT), along with RB Deuce McAllister getting a 1-yard TD run. San Diego would answer with QB Philip Rivers completing a 12-yard TD pass to RB LaDainian Tomlinson, yet the Saints increased their lead as Brees completed a 30-yard TD pass to WR Lance Moore. The Chargers closed out the half as Rivers completed a 12-yard TD pass to TE Antonio Gates.

In the third quarter, New Orleans added on to their lead as Brees completed a 1-yard TD pass to TE Mark Campbell, yet San Diego continued to hang around as Kaeding got a 24-yard field goal. In the fourth quarter, the Saints continued its scoring with FB Mike Karney getting a 1-yard TD run. The Chargers tried to rally as Kaeding nailed a 31-yard field goal, Rivers completed a 14-yard TD run to

WR Vincent Jackson, and Brees giving San Diego a safety by throwing an incomplete pass into the back of his own end zone. Fortunately, New Orleans' defense held on for the victory.

With the win, the Saints went into their bye week at 4-4.

Week 10: at Atlanta Falcons

Coming off their bye week, the Saints flew to the Georgia Dome for a Week 10 NFC South duel with the Atlanta Falcons. In the first quarter, New Orleans trailed early as Falcons QB Matt Ryan completed a 16-yard TD pass to WR Roddy White. The Saints responded with rookie kicker Garrett Hartley getting a 24-yard field goal. In the second quarter, Atlanta answered with RB Michael Turner getting a 2-yard TD run. New Orleans would reply with Hartley making a 44-yard field goal. The Falcons would end the half with kicker Jason Elam getting a 22-yard field goal.

In the third quarter, Atlanta increased its lead with Elam nailing a 27-yard field goal. In the fourth quarter, the Falcons began to pull away as Ryan completed a 67-yard TD pass to RB Jerious Norwood. The Saints tried to rally as QB Drew Brees completed a 15-yard TD pass to RB Deuce McAllister, but Atlanta sealed the win with CB Chevis Jackson returning an interception 95 yards for a touchdown. New Orleans would end the game with a meaningless 32-yard TD pass from Brees to WR Lance Moore.

With the regular loss, not only did the Saints fall to 4-5, but their 4-game winning streak against the Falcons was snapped.

Week 11: at Kansas City Chiefs

Hoping to rebound from their divisional road loss to the Falcons, the Saints flew to Arrowhead Stadium for a Week 11 interconference duel with the Kansas City Chiefs. In the first quarter, New Orleans trailed early as Chiefs QB Tyler Thigpen completed a 6-yard TD pass to WR Dwayne Bowe. The Saints would respond with rookie kicker Garrett Hartley getting a 30-yard field goal. In the second quarter, New Orleans took the lead as RB Deuce McAllister got a 1-yard TD run. Kansas City would answer with kicker Connor Barth getting a 20-yard field goal, yet the Saints closed out the half with Hartley making a 23-yard field goal.

In the third quarter, New Orleans increased their lead as QB Drew Brees completed a 47-yard TD pass to WR Lance Moore. The Chiefs would reply with Barth getting a 21-yard field goal, yet the Saints answered with RB Pierre Thomas getting a 1-yard TD run. In the fourth quarter, Kansas City tried to rally as Thigpen hooked up with Bowe again on a 5-yard TD pass, yet New Orleans closed out the game as Hartley nailed a 35-yard field goal.

With the win, the Saints improved to 5-5.

Week 12: vs. Green Bay Packers

Coming off their road win over the Chiefs, the Saints went home for a Week 12 MNF duel with the Green Bay Packers. In the first quarter, New Orleans trailed early as Packers FB John Kuhn got a 1-yard TD run. The Saints would take the lead as QB Drew Brees completed a 70-yard TD pass to WR Lance Moore (which gave him his 9th-straight game of throwing a pass of 40+ yards, an NFL record), while RB Pierre Thomas got a 4-yard TD run. In the second quarter, Green Bay responded with QB Aaron Rodgers completing a 7-yard TD pass to WR Greg Jennings. New Orleans would answer with Brees hooking up with Moore again on a 14-yard TD pass. The Packers would tie the game as Rodgers got a 10-yard TD run, yet New Orleans regained the lead prior to halftime as rookie kicker Garrett Hartley made a 30-yard field goal.

In the third quarter, the Saints' offense exploded as Brees completed a 16-yard TD pass to TE Billy Miller, RB Deuce McAllister got a 3-yard TD run (which was his 49th career touchdown, making him the franchise's all-time career TD leader), and Brees completed a 70-yard TD pass to WR Marques Colston. In the fourth quarter, Green Bay tried to rally as Rodgers completed a 4-yard TD pass and a 2-point conversion pass to WR Ruvell Martin. Afterwards, New Orleans closed out the game with Thomas' 31-yard TD run (with a failed 2-point conversion).

With the win, the Saints kept their playoff hopes alive at 6-5.

Week 13: at Tampa Bay Buccaneers

Coming off their Monday Night home win over the Packers, the Saints flew to Raymond James Stadium for a Week 13 NFC South rematch with the Tampa Bay Buccaneers. In the first quarter, New Orleans struck first as rookie kicker Garrett Hartley got a 47-yard field goal. In the second quarter, the Buccaneers took the lead as kicker Matt Bryant got a 38-yard and a 23-yard field goal. The Saints would regain the lead as QB Drew Brees completed a 13-yard TD pass to WR Lance Moore.

In the third quarter, Tampa Bay regained the lead as RB Carnell "Cadillac" Williams got an 8-yard TD run, along with QB Jeff Garcia completing a 39-yard TD pass to WR Antonio Bryant. In the fourth quarter, New Orleans would tie the game as Brees completed a 20-yard TD pass to RB Pierre Thomas, along with Hartley getting a 43-yard field goal. However, the Buccaneers regained the lead as Bryant nailed a 37-yard field goal. The Saints tried to rally, but Brees' third interception prevented any hope of a comeback.

With the heart-breaking loss, New Orleans fell to 6-6.

Week 14: vs. Atlanta Falcons

Coming off a heartbreaking loss to Tampa Bay, the New Orleans Saints returned home to host the Atlanta Falcons. The Falcons appeared to be on the move on their first drive, but they came up empty after Saints cornerback Jason David intercepted Falcons rookie quarterback Matt Ryan at the Saints' 26-yard line. From there, it took New Orleans only three plays to get into the end zone as Reggie Bush ran for 43 yards and then caught a 5-yard touchdown pass from Drew Brees for the only score of the quarter.

In the second quarter, the Saints added to their lead with a 26-yard field goal from Garrett Hartley. The Atlanta offense finally woke up from there as Ryan completed a 59-yard pass to Roddy White, leading to an eventual 5-yard touchdown run by Michael Turner, cutting the deficit to 10-7. New Orleans would respond with a 10-play, 3:39 drive that culminated in a 46-yard field goal by Hartley, extending the Saints' lead to 13-7. Ryan then completed five of six passes on the Falcons' next drive, the last of which was a 2-yard touchdown pass to Brian Finneran, giving the Falcons a 14-13 lead. The Saints would then use the final 2:13 of the half to drive to the Falcons' 7-yard line, and closed out the half on a 25-yard field goal by Hartley to give New Orleans a 16-14 halftime lead.

After an exchange of punts to begin the second half, Atlanta drove down to the Saints' 5-yard line by virtue of a long 18-play, 9:15 drive, only to settle for a 23-yard field goal by Jason Elam, which nevertheless gave the Falcons a 17-16 lead. New Orleans responded with an 11-play drive bridging the third and fourth quarters, which ended with Brees' 7-yard touchdown pass to Pierre Thomas, with a failed two-point conversion. The Falcons then marched 73 yards in 11 plays, the last being a 12-yard touchdown scramble by Ryan, plus a successful two-point conversion to Michael Jenkins. But thanks to an 88-yard return by Thomas on the ensuing kickoff, the Saints' drive started off at the Falcons' 16-yard line. With the Saints facing 4th-and 1 at the 7 yard line, New Orleans coach Sean Payton elected to go for it rather than attempt a game-tying 25-yard field goal. Fullback Mike Karney came through for the Saints, getting a first down, and then Thomas gave the Saints a 29-25 lead with a 5-yard touchdown run. The Falcons could not get past their own 35-yard line on the ensuing drive, and they chose to punt the ball back to the Saints' offense, which ran out the clock.

With the win, the Saints kept their slim playoff hopes alive at 7-6. Pierre Thomas piled up 197 all-purpose yards, including 109 yards from scrimmage, 102 of it rushing. This was also the second time in a row that the Saints followed a heartbreaking loss to the Buccaneers with a win over the Falcons.

Week 15: at Chicago Bears

With a divisional home win to the Falcons behind them, the Saints flew to Soldier Field for a Week 15 Thursday night battle with the Chicago Bears. New Orleans immediately trailed as in the first quarter, as Bears safety Danieal Manning returned the game's opening kickoff 83 yards for a touchdown. The Saints would answer with quarterback Drew Brees' 2-yard touchdown pass to running back Pierre

Thomas, but Chicago struck right back as running back Matt Forté got a 1-yard touchdown run, along with quarterback Kyle Orton getting a 6-yard touchdown run.

The Saints would begin to rally in the third quarter, as Thomas got a 42-yard touchdown run. In the fourth quarter, New Orleans took the lead as kicker Garrett Hartley got a 30-yard field goal, along with Brees completing an 11-yard touchdown pass to wide receiver Marques Colston. However, the Bears tied the game as kicker Robbie Gould made a 28-yard field goal. In overtime, Chicago sealed New Orleans' fate as Gould nailed the game-winning 35-yard field goal.

With the heart-breaking loss, not only did the Saints fall to 7-7, but it knocked them out of playoff contention after Atlanta's 13-10 overtime win over Tampa Bay on December 14.

Week 16: at Detroit Lions

Coming off their loss to the Bears, the Saints flew to Ford Field for a Week 16 duel with the winless Detroit Lions. New Orleans would get the early first quarter lead as wide receiver Robert Meachem got a 20-yard touchdown run, followed by running back Deuce McAllister's 2-yard touchdown run. In the second quarter, the Lions would answer with running back Kevin Smith getting a 1-yard touchdown run, yet the Saints would answer with running back Mike Bell's 1-yard touchdown run, followed by running back Pierre Thomas's 2-yard touchdown run. New Orleans would close out the game's scoring with quarterback Drew Brees completing a 6-yard and a 3-yard touchdown pass to wide receiver Marques Colston.

With the win, the Saints improved to 8-7.

Week 17: vs. Carolina Panthers

Coming off their road win over the Lions, the Saints closed out their season at home in a Week 17 NFC South rematch with the Carolina Panthers. New Orleans would trail early in the first quarter as Panthers kicker John Kasay got a 45-yard and a 26-yard field goal. In the second quarter, the Saints would respond as rookie kicker Garrett Hartley made a 21-yard field goal, yet Carolina answered with Kasay's 34-yard field goal, quarterback Jake Delhomme's 8-yard touchdown pass to wide receiver Muhsin Muhammad, and cornerback Dante Wesley's 12-yard fumble return for a touchdown. New Orleans would close out the half with quarterback Drew Brees completing a 26-yard touchdown pass to wide receiver Marques Colston.

The Panthers would add on to their lead in the third quarter as running back Jonathan Stewart got a 2-yard touchdown run. In the fourth quarter, the Saints rallied to take the lead as Brees completed a 7-yard touchdown pass to wide receiver Robert Meachem, along with a 9-yard and a 13-yard touchdown pass to wide receiver Lance Moore. However, Carolina took the lead for good as Kasay nailed the game-winning 42-yard field goal.

With the loss, New Orleans ended their season at 8-8.

Despite falling 16 yards shy of surpassing Dan Marino for the most single-season passing yards, Brees (30/49 for 386 yards, 4 TDs, 1 INT) would join Marino as the only quarterbacks to throw for 5,000+ yards in a season (5,069).

Statistics

Final Stats

Source: ESPN

Passing

Player	G	QB Rat.	Comp.	Att.	Pct.	Yards	TD	INT	Long	Sack
Drew Brees	16	96.2	413	635	65.0	5069	34	17	84	13
Lance Moore	0	0.0	0	1	0	0.0	0	1	0	0

Rushing

Player	Att.	Yards	Avg.	Long	TD
Reggie Bush	106	404	3.8	43	2
Deuce McAllister	107	418	3.9	19	5
Pierre Thomas	129	625	4.8	42	9
Drew Brees	22	-1	0.0	9	0
Aaron Stecker	8	43	5.4	12	0
Mike Karney	8	10	1.3	3	2
Mike Bell	13	42	3.2	15	1
Devery Henderson	4	33	8.3	30	0
Robert Meachem	1	20	20.0	20	1

Receiving

Player	Rec.	Yards	Avg.	Long	TD
Reggie Bush	52	440	8.5	42	4
Lance Moore	79	928	11.7	70	10
Jeremy Shockey	50	483	9.7	26	0
Devery Henderson	32	793	24.8	84	3
David Patten	11	162	14.7	39	1
Mark Campbell	12	121	10.1	29	2
Robert Meachem	12	289	24.1	74	3
Billy Miller	45	579	12.9	41	1
Pierre Thomas	31	284	9.2	24	3
Mike Karney	9	18	2.0	7	0
Marques Colston	47	760	16.2	70	5
Deuce McAllister	18	128	7.1	20	1
Olaniyi Sobomehin	2	8	4.0	10	0
Aaron Stecker	9	52	5.8	12	1
Sean Ryan	2	7	3.5	5	0
Buck Ortega	1	3	3	3	0
Mike Bell	1	14	14	14	0

Place Kicking

Player	1-19 A	1-19 M	20-29 A	20-29 M	30-39 A	30-39 M	40-49 A	40-49 M	+50 A	+50 M	LNG	TOT	PCT	XPM/A	XP PCT	PTS
Martín Gramática	0	0	0	0	3	3	5	2	2	1	53	6/10	60%	16/16	100%	34
Taylor Mehlhaff	0	0	1	1	2	1	1	1	0	0	44	3/4	75%	9/10	90%	18
Garrett Hartley	0	0	5	5	4	4	4	4	0	0	47	13/13	100%	28/28	100%	67

Punting

Player	Punt	Yards	Avg.	In20	TB	Long
Steve Weatherford	26	1094	42.1	5	3	61
Ben Graham	3	126	42	1	0	44
Glenn Pakulak	24	1144	47.7	3	2	70

2009 New Orleans Saints season

The **2009 New Orleans Saints season** is the franchise's 43rd season in the National Football League (NFL) and the most successful in franchise history in which they won Super Bowl XLIV. The Saints recorded a franchise record 13 victories, an improvement on their 8–8 record and fourth place finish in the National Football Conference (NFC)'s southern division from 2008. As a result, the Saints returned to the playoffs for the first time since 2006. For head coach Sean Payton, this was his fourth season with the franchise, commanding a club overall record of 36–24. After becoming 8–0 with their win over the Carolina Panthers on November 8, it marked the Saints' best start to a season in its franchise history. They would go on to set the record for the longest undefeated season opening (13–0) by an NFC team since the AFL–NFL merger, eclipsing the previous record (12–0) held by the 1985 Chicago Bears.

Although losing the last three games of the season to finish 13–3, the team clinched a playoff berth, a bye in the first round of the playoffs, and (for the first time in Saints franchise history) the top seed in the NFC. The Saints defeated the Arizona Cardinals in the NFC Divisional playoffs, and proceeded to host the NFC Championship Game for the first time at home in franchise history, second in franchise history, and second in the past four seasons. There, they defeated the Minnesota Vikings to face the Indianapolis Colts at Super Bowl XLIV in the franchise's first-ever Super Bowl appearance, which they won to give the city of New Orleans its first world championship.

Although five Saints were elected to the Pro Bowl (with two others added as injury replacements), since the game was held one week prior to Super Bowl XLIV, they did not participate.

Offseason

Staff changes

- Bill Johnson was named the defensive line coach.
- Gary Gibbs was replaced by Gregg Williams as the defensive coordinator on January 15, 2009 after Gibbs was released on January 7, 2009.
- On January 12, 2009, Pete Carmichael, Jr. replaced Doug Marrone as the offensive coordinator after Marrone had resigned from his position in December 2008; Aaron Kromer was named the offensive line coach/running game, and as a result, Bret Ingalls replaced him as the running backs coach; Joe Lombardi was named the quarterbacks coach.

Signings

Pos.	Player	Date	Notes
CB	Jabari Greer	March 4, 2009	
FB	Heath Evans	March 5, 2009	
DL	Paul Spicer	March 17, 2009	
C	Nick Leckey	March 17, 2009	
TE	Darnell Dinkins	March 18, 2009	
S	Darren Sharper	March 18, 2009	
S	Pierson Prioleau	March 26, 2009	
DT	Roderick Coleman	March 27, 2009	
LB	Anthony Waters	April 15, 2009	
DB	Malcolm Jenkins	April 25, 2009	#14 overall 2009 NFL Draft pick

S	Chip Vaughn	April 26, 2009	#116 overall 2009 NFL Draft pick
LB	Stanley Arnoux	April 26, 2009	#118 overall 2009 NFL Draft pick
P	Thomas Morstead	April 26, 2009	#164th overall 2009 NFL Draft pick, acquired as part of a pick trade with the Philadelphia Eagles
DT	Anthony Hargrove	May 18, 2009	
RB	Deuce McAllister	January 15, 2010	Resigned to active roster and named honorary team captain.

Departures

Pos.	Player	Date	Notes
WR	David Patten	February 12, 2009	Placed on waived-injured list
RB	Deuce McAllister	February 17, 2009	Placed on *waived-injured list*
CB	Mike McKenzie	March 19, 2009	Placed on *waived-injured* list
DT	Brian Young	April 28, 2009	Placed on *waived-injured* list
DT	Hollis Thomas	April 29, 2009	Placed on *waived-injured* list
RB	Deuce McAllister	January 19, 2010	Retires from football and placed on *reserve-retired list*

Personnel

Final roster

New Orleans Saints 2009 final roster

Quarterbacks

- 9 Drew Brees
- 11 Mark Brunell
- 10 *Chase Daniel*

Running Backs

- 21 Mike Bell
- 25 Reggie Bush PR
- 36 Kyle Eckel FB
- 30 Lynell Hamilton
- 23 Pierre Thomas

Wide Receivers

- 87 Adrian Arrington
- 12 Marques Colston
- 19 Devery Henderson
- 17 Robert Meachem
- 16 Lance Moore
- 15 Courtney Roby KR

Tight Ends

- 80 Darnell Dinkins
- 84 Tory Humphrey
- 88 Jeremy Shockey
- 85 David Thomas FB

Offensive Linemen

- 74 Jermon Bushrod T
- 73 Jahri Evans G
- 76 Jonathan Goodwin C
- 60 Nick Leckey C
- 67 Jamar Nesbit G
- 77 Carl Nicks G
- 78 Jon Stinchcomb T
- 64 Zach Strief T

Defensive Linemen

- 92 Remi Ayodele DT
- 97 Jeff Charleston DE
- 98 Sedrick Ellis DT
- 69 Anthony Hargrove DT
- 93 Bobby McCray DE
- 90 DeMario Pressley DT
- 91 Will Smith DE
- 96 Paul Spicer DE

Linebackers

- 52 *Jonathan Casillas* OLB
- 54 Troy Evans OLB
- 55 Scott Fujita OLB
- 50 Marvin Mitchell ILB
- 58 Scott Shanle OLB
- 51 Jonathan Vilma ILB
- 59 Anthony Waters OLB

Defensive Backs

- 20 Randall Gay CB
- 33 Jabari Greer CB
- 41 Roman Harper SS
- 27 *Malcolm Jenkins* CB
- 22 Tracy Porter CB
- 31 Pierson Prioleau SS
- 39 Chris Reis SS
- 42 Darren Sharper FS
- 28 Usama Young FS

Special Teams

- 5 Garrett Hartley K
- 57 Jason Kyle LS
- 6 *Thomas Morstead* P

Reserve Lists

- 99 *Stanley Arnoux* ILB (IR)
- 70 Jammal Brown OT (IR)
- 86 Dan Campbell TE (IR)
- 71 Kendrick Clancy DT (IR)
- 56 Jo-Lonn Dunbar OLB (IR)
- 44 Heath Evans FB (IR)
- 94 Charles Grant DE (IR)
- 13 Rod Harper WR (IR)
- 35 *Reggie Jones* CB (IR)
- 95 Rodney Leisle DT (IR)
- 46 *Marcus Mailei* FB (IR)
- 83 Billy Miller TE (IR)
- 53 Mark Simoneau ILB (IR)
- 24 Leigh Torrence CB (IR)
- 37 *Chip Vaughn* FS (IR)
- -- D'Juan Woods WR (IR)

Practice Squad

- 72 Tim Duckworth G
- 38 Greg Fassitt CB
- 63 *Marlon Favorite* DT
- 75 Na'Shan Goddard T
- 66 *Earl Heyman* DT
- 82 *Tyler Lorenzen* TE
- 79 *Jermey Parnell* OT
- 29 Glenn Sharpe CB

Rookies in italics
53 Active, 16 Inactive, 8 PS

Coaching staff

New Orleans Saints 2009 staff	
Front Office	**Defensive Coaches**
• Owner – Tom Benson	• Defensive Coordinator – Gregg Williams
• Owner/Executive Vice President – Rita Benson LeBlanc	• Defensive Line – Bill Johnson
• Executive Vice President/General Manager – Mickey Loomis	• Assistant Defensive Line – Travis Jones
• Director of Football Administration – Khai Harley	• Secondary – Dennis Allen
• Director of Pro Scouting – Ryan Pace	• Assistant Secondary – Tony Oden
• Director of College Scouting – Rick Reiprish	• Defensive Assistant/Linebackers – Adam Zimmer
• Assistant Director of College Scouting – Brian Adams	**Special Teams Coaches**
Head Coaches	• Special Teams Coordinator – Greg McMahon
• Head Coach – Sean Payton	• Assistant Special Teams – Mike Mallory
• Assistant Head Coach/Linebackers – Joe Vitt	**Strength and Conditioning**
Offensive Coaches	• Head Strength and Conditioning – Dan Dalrymple
• Offensive Coordinator – Pete Carmichael, Jr.	• Assistant Strength and Conditioning – Adam Bailey
• Quarterbacks – Joe Lombardi	• Strength and Conditioning Assistant – Charles Byrd
• Running Backs – Bret Ingalls	**Coaching Assistants**
• Wide Receivers – Curtis Johnson	• Mike Cerullo, Blake Williams
• Tight Ends – Terry Malone	
• Offensive Line/Running Game – Aaron Kromer	
• Offensive Assistant/Assistant Player Programs – Carter Sheridan	

Preseason

Week	Date	Kickoff	Opponent	Results		Game Site	TV	NFL Recap
				Final score	Team record			
1	Friday, Aug. 14	7:00pm CDT	Cincinnati Bengals	W 17–7	1–0	Louisiana Superdome	Fox	[1]
2	Saturday, Aug. 22	7:00pm CDT	at Houston Texans	W 38–14	2–0	Reliant Stadium	KTRK-TV	[2]
3	Saturday, Aug. 29	3:00pm CDT	at Oakland Raiders	W 45–7	3–0	Oakland-Alameda County Coliseum	Local	[3]
4	Thursday, Sept. 3	7:00pm CDT	Miami Dolphins	L 10–7	3–1	Louisiana Superdome		

Regular season

Schedule

The Saints' regular season schedule was released on April 14, 2009.

Week	Date	Kickoff	Opponent	Results		Game Site	TV	NFL.com Recap
				Final score	Team record			
1	September 13	12:00pm CDT	Detroit Lions	**W** 45–27	1–0	Louisiana Superdome	Fox	Recap [4]
2	September 20	12:00pm CDT	at Philadelphia Eagles	**W** 48–22	2–0	Lincoln Financial Field	Fox	Recap [5]
3	September 27	3:05pm CDT	at Buffalo Bills	W 27–7	3–0	Ralph Wilson Stadium	Fox	Recap [6]
4	October 4	3:05pm CDT	New York Jets	**W** 24–10	4–0	Louisiana Superdome	CBS	Recap [7]
5			*Bye*					
6	October 18	12:00pm CDT	New York Giants	**W** 48–27	5–0	Louisiana Superdome	Fox	Recap [8]
7	October 25	3:15pm CDT	at Miami Dolphins	**W** 46–34	6–0	Landshark Stadium	Fox	Recap [9]
8	Nov. 2 *(Monday)*	7:30pm CST	**Atlanta Falcons**	**W** 35–27	7–0	Louisiana Superdome	ESPN	Recap [10]
9	November 8	3:05pm CST	**Carolina Panthers**	**W** 30–20	8–0	Louisiana Superdome	Fox	Recap [11]
10	November 15	12:00pm CST	at St. Louis Rams	**W** 28–23	9–0	Edward Jones Dome	Fox	Recap [12]
11	November 22	12:00pm CST	at **Tampa Bay Buccaneers**	W 38–7	10–0	Raymond James Stadium	Fox	Recap [13]
12	November 30 *(Monday)*	7:30pm CST	New England Patriots	**W** 38–17	11–0	Louisiana Superdome	ESPN	Recap [14]
13	December 6	12:00pm CST	at Washington Redskins	**W** 33–30 (OT)	12–0	FedEx Field	Fox	Recap [15]
14	December 13	12:00pm CST	at **Atlanta Falcons**	**W** 26–23	13–0	Georgia Dome	Fox	Recap [16]

15	Dec. 19 (Saturday)	7:20pm CST	Dallas Cowboys	L 24–17	13–1	Louisiana Superdome	NFLN	Recap [17]
16	December 27	12:00pm CST	**Tampa Bay Buccaneers**	L 20–17 (OT)	13–2	Louisiana Superdome	Fox	Recap [18]
17	January 3, 2010	12:00pm CST	at **Carolina Panthers**	L 23–10	13–3	Bank of America Stadium	Fox	Recap [19]
NOTE: Division games are in **bold** text.								

Game summaries

Week 1: vs. Detroit Lions

The Saints began their season with a Week 1 duel with the Detroit Lions. New Orleans would get off to a fast start in the first quarter as quarterback Drew Brees completed a 9-yard touchdown pass to wide receiver Marques Colston and a 39-yard touchdown pass to wide receiver Robert Meachem. The Lions would answer with kicker Jason Hanson getting a 47-yard field goal. In the second quarter, Detroit came closer as running back Kevin Smith got a 4-yard touchdown run. The Saints would reply with Brees completing a 1-yard and a 15-yard touchdown pass to tight end Jeremy Shockey.

The Lions tried to catch up in the third quarter as quarterback Matthew Stafford got a 1-yard touchdown run, yet New Orleans answered with kicker John Carney making a 39-yard field goal. Detroit would respond with Hanson nailing a 24-yard field goal, while the Saints kept pounding away as Brees completed a 58-yard touchdown pass to wide receiver Devery Henderson. The Lions would close out the period with safety Louis Delmas returning a fumble 65 yards for a touchdown. In the fourth quarter, New Orleans closed out the game as Brees completed a 13-yard touchdown pass to fullback Heath Evans.

With the win, not only did the Saints begin their season at 1–0, but Brees (26-of-34, 358 yards, 6 TDs, 1 INT) became the very first quarterback to throw 6 TD passes in an opening day game, as well as tying Billy Kilmer's franchise record for touchdown passes in a game.

Week 2: at Philadelphia Eagles

Coming off their win over the Lions, the Saints flew to Lincoln Financial Field for a Week 2 duel with the Philadelphia Eagles. In the first quarter, New Orleans drew first blood as quarterback Drew Brees completed a 15-yard touchdown pass to wide receiver Marques Colston. The Eagles answered with quarterback Kevin Kolb (in his first start as the Eagles' quarterback) completing a 71-yard touchdown pass to wide receiver DeSean Jackson, yet the Saints replied with kicker John Carney making a 23-yard field goal. In the second quarter, Philadelphia tied the game as kicker David Akers got a 23-yard field goal. New Orleans answered with Brees completing a 25-yard touchdown pass to Colston. The Eagles closed out the half as Akers made a 32-yard field goal.

In the third quarter, the Saints began to take command as Brees completed an 11-yard touchdown pass to fullback Heath Evans, along with running back Mike Bell getting a 7-yard touchdown run and Carney nailing a 25-yard field goal. The Eagles answered with Kolb completing a 3-yard touchdown pass to wide receiver Jason Avant. In the fourth quarter, New Orleans kept up its domination as running back Reggie Bush got a 19-yard touchdown. Philadelphia drove to the Saints' 5 yard line but could not score and the drive ended on downs; the Saints were then unable to move the ball, and rather than punting out of their own end zone, they opted to have Brees throw the ball out of the end zone for an intentional safety. After the ensuing free kick, the Eagles again drove deep into Saints territory, but again failed to score, as Kolb threw an interception which safety Darren Sharper returned 97 yards for a touchdown.

With the win, the Saints improved to 2–0.

Week 3: at Buffalo Bills

Coming off their win over the Eagles, the Saints flew to Ralph Wilson Stadium for a Week 3 interconference duel with the Buffalo Bills. New Orleans would make an immediate impact in the first quarter with running back Lynell Hamilton's 1-yard touchdown run. The Bills would answer in the second quarter when a fake field goal attempt, punter Brian Moorman would complete a 25-yard touchdown pass to defensive end Ryan Denney. The Saints would close out the half with kicker John Carney's 27-yard field goal. After a scoreless third quarter, New Orleans would take control in the fourth quarter with running back Pierre Thomas' 34-yard touchdown run, Carney's 35-yard field goal, and Thomas' 19-yard touchdown run.

With the win, the Saints improved to 3–0.

Week 4: vs. New York Jets

Coming off their road win over the Bills, the Saints went home for a Week 4 interconference duel with the New York Jets. New Orleans would deliver the game's first points as kicker John Carney got a 34-yard field goal. In the second quarter, the defense went to work. Safety Darren Sharper would return an interception 99 yards for a touchdown, followed by defensive end Will Smith forcing an endzone fumble by sacking Jets quarterback Mark Sanchez, which allowed defensive tackle Remi Ayodele to land on the ball for a touchdown. Afterwards, New York closed out the half with kicker Jay Feely's 38-yard field goal.

The Jets would begin a comeback attempt in the third quarter with running back Thomas Jones getting a 15-yard touchdown run. Afterwards, the Saints would close out the game with running back Pierre Thomas' 1-yard touchdown and the defense making an impressive stand.

With the win, New Orleans would enter its bye week at 4–0.

Week 6: vs. New York Giants

Coming off their bye week, the Saints stayed at home for a huge Week 6 game in a "Battle of The Unbeatens" against the New York Giants. New Orleans' offense would roar out of the gates in the first quarter with running back Mike Bell's 2-yard touchdown run and quarterback Drew Brees' 1-yard touchdown pass to former Giants tight end Jeremy Shockey. New York would then close out the opening quarter with a 49-yard field goal from kicker Lawrence Tynes. The Saints' high-powered offense continued to heat up in the second quarter as Brees completed a 36-yard touchdown pass to wide receiver Robert Meachem. The Giants would try to keep up as running back Ahmad Bradshaw got a 10-yard touchdown run, yet New Orleans answered with Brees hooking up with wide receiver Lance Moore on a 12-yard touchdown run. New York continued to stay persistent as quarterback Eli Manning completed a 15-yard touchdown pass to wide receiver Mario Manningham, yet the Saints closed out the half with a 7-yard touchdown run from running back Reggie Bush.

New Orleans would solidify its lead in the third quarter with Brees finding wide receiver Marques Colston on a 12-yard touchdown pass. The Giants opened the fourth quarter with Tynes booting a 38-yard field goal, yet the Saints ended its dominating run with fullback Heath Evans getting a 2-yard touchdown run. New York would then close out the game's scoring with quarterback David Carr completing a 37-yard touchdown pass to wide receiver Hakeem Nicks.

With the win, New Orleans improved to 5–0.

Week 7: at Miami Dolphins

In Week 7, the Saints traveled to South Florida to continue their interconference series against the Dolphins. Miami jumped out to a 24–3 lead by the second quarter, with former Saint first-rounder and Heisman winner Ricky Williams scoring on runs of 4 and 68 yards, and Ronnie Brown added a touchdown run of 8 yards in the second quarter. Despite being behind for the first time in the season, the Saints gained momentum when Drew Brees scored on a quarterback sneak to end the first half and cap a 1:36 drive of 51 yards. In the second half, the Saints scored on a 42 yard interception return by Darren Sharper in the third, but Dan Carpenter added a second field goal to push the lead back to ten points. The Saints responded with a 10 yard Brees-Colston connection, but Ricky Williams answered with another 4 yard rushing score to make the score 34–24. The Saints completed their comeback in the fourth quarter, first with Reggie Bush scoring on a reverse from 10 yards out, then with Brees scoring his second rush TD from 2. Though John Carney missed the extra point, he later hit a field goal from 20 yards, and Tracy Porter sealed the comeback with a 54 yard interception return. The Saints outscored Miami 22–0 in the fourth quarter, and 36–10 for the second half.

The Saints improved to 6–0 with the win.

Week 8: vs. Atlanta Falcons

Coming off their comeback road win over the Dolphins, the Saints went home for a Week 8 NFC South duel with the Atlanta Falcons on Monday night. New Orleans would initially trail in the first quarter as Falcons running back Michael Turner got a 13-yard touchdown run, yet the Saints answered with running back Pierre Thomas getting a 22-yard touchdown run. Atlanta would come right back as quarterback Drew Brees was sacked by free safety Thomas DeCoud, causing him to fumble and allow defensive end Kroy Biermann to return the ball 4 yards for a touchdown. In the second quarter, New Orleans would go on a rampage with Brees' 18-yard touchdown pass to wide receiver Marques Colston, running back Reggie Bush's 1-yard touchdown run, and cornerback Jabari Greer's 48-yard interception return for a touchdown.

However, the Falcons began to get back into the game with quarterback Matt Ryan finding wide receiver Roddy White on a 68-yard touchdown pass in the third quarter, followed by kicker Jason Elam booting a 25-yard field goal. Fortunately, cornerback Tracy Porter's key interception (helped from linebacker Jonathan Vilma's tip) lead to Brees finding Thomas on a 1-yard touchdown pass. Even though Atlanta crept closer with Elam nailing a 40-yard field goal and recovering an onside kick, free safety Darren Sharper's interception sealed the tight victory.

With the win, the Saints improved to 7–0 (tying their best start in 1991).

Week 9: vs. Carolina Panthers

Coming off their Monday night win over the Falcons, the Saints stayed at home for a Week 9 NFC South duel with the Carolina Panthers. New Orleans would trail in the first quarter as Panthers running back DeAngelo Williams got a 66-yard and a 7-yard touchdown run. In the second quarter, the Saints got on the board with a 23-yard field goal from kicker John Carney. Carolina would reply with kicker John Kasay getting a 32-yard field goal, yet New Orleans would close out the half with Carney's 25-yard field goal.

In the third quarter, the Saints crept closer with a 10-yard touchdown by running back Pierre Thomas. The Panthers would reply with Kasay nailing a 25-yard field goal, yet New Orleans would close out the period with quarterback Drew Brees' 54-yard touchdown pass to wide receiver Robert Meachem. Afterwards, the Saints took command in the fourth quarter as Carney booted a 40-yard field goal, followed by defensive tackle Anthony Hargrove forcing Williams into a fumble and recovering it for a 1-yard touchdown run.

With the win, the Saints improved to 8–0, which is the team's best start in franchise history.

Week 10: at St. Louis Rams

Coming off their divisional home win over the Panthers, the Saints flew to the Edward Jones Dome for a Week 10 duel with the St. Louis Rams. After a scoreless first quarter, New Orleans got the game's inaugural points in the second quarter with running back Reggie Bush getting a 3-yard touchdown run. The Rams would respond with quarterback Marc Bulger completing a 29-yard touchdown pass to wide receiver Donnie Avery. New Orleans would answer with quarterback Drew Brees hooking up with Bush on a 15-yard touchdown pass, yet St. Louis would close out the half with a 2-yard touchdown run from running back Steven Jackson.

The Saints would begin the third quarter with wide receiver Courtney Roby returning the second half's opening kickoff 97 yards for a touchdown. The Rams would stay close with kicker Josh Brown nailing a 32-yard field goal. New Orleans would extend their lead in the fourth quarter Brees finding wide receiver Robert Meachem on a 27-yard touchdown pass. St. Louis tried to catch up as Bulger found Avery again on a 19-yard touchdown pass (with a failed 2-point conversion), yet the defense prevented the Rams from getting any closer.

With the win, the Saints improved to 9–0.

Week 11: at Tampa Bay Buccaneers

Coming off a tough road win against the Rams, the Saints went to Raymond James Stadium for a Week 11 duel against the Tampa Bay Buccaneers. After a quick first quarter Tampa Bay touchdown from rookie quarterback Josh Freeman to Micheal Clayton to cap a 95-yard drive, the Bucs showed how the Saints struggled defensively. The Bucs looked to improve on their next drive by moving the ball with running backs Carnell Williams and Ernest Graham. The Saints would answer defensively as they took advantage of numerous mistakes by rookie Tampa Bay quarterback Josh Freeman.

Drew Brees passed for 187 yards and three touchdowns. He connected with Robert Meacham for a 4-yard touchdown catch and a 6-yard touchdown catch, and to tight end David Thomas for a 11-yard touchdown. Pressure on the young Freeman from the Saints forced him to throw 3-interceptions and a fumble, allowing the Saints to take more control during the second half. The Saints would close out the game in the with two scores from running back Mike Bell from 3 yards and one yard out.

With the win, the Saints improved to 10–0.

Week 12: vs. New England Patriots

The Saints returned to the Dome for possibly the most hyped game in recent team history, a Monday Night showdown in front of 70,768 with the 7–3 Patriots, winners of 3 Super Bowls in this decade. The Saints came out firing from the start with a 33 yard completion from Brees to Devery Henderson. The drive resulted in a John Carney FG from 30 yards. The Pats stormed back on the next drive, converting twice on 4th-and-1, the second being Laurence Maroney's 4 yard TD run to put New England in the lead. On New England's next drive, Tom Brady was intercepted by a healthy and re-signed Mike

McKenzie, leading to a TD from Brees to Pierre Thomas on a 18 yard swing pass. Forcing the Pats to punt again, Drew Brees found a wide-open Henderson on the next play, who waltzed into the endzone on a 75 yard reception to make it 17–7. The Patriots scored again on a 38 yard FG by Stephen Gostkowski. Drew Brees made it 24–10 on a 38 yarder to Robert Meachem, which was set up by a 25 yard catch by former Patriots TE David Thomas, and Gostkowski missed a 50 yard FG wide to close out the half.

On the Pats first play of the third quarter, Scott Fujita forced Maroney to fumble, and Sedrick Ellis recovered the ball. However, Maroney forced Ellis to fumble, and Wes Welker recovered the ball on the New England 19. Brady then drove New England downfield, including a 47 yarder to Randy Moss, and Maroney scored his second rush TD from two yards. On the next offensive play, Marques Colston turns a 10 yard catch into a 68 yard gain to the Patriots 6, and New Orleans gets another touchdown via a two yard catch by backup TE Darnell Dinkins. In the fourth quarter, Brees hits Colston from 20 yards for his 5th passing TD of the game, and the game was sealed when Sharper got his 8th interception of the year, and Brady is pulled with 5:28 to go, replaced by backup Brad Hoyer.

With the win, the Saints improve to 11–0. Drew Brees completed 18 of 23 passes for a season-high 371 yards, five touchdowns and his first-ever perfect passer rating of 158.3, and became the first to throw 5 TDs against a Bill Belichek-coached team.

The television broadcast of the game on ESPN's *Monday Night Football* was the second-most-watched cable telecast of all time.

Week 13: at Washington Redskins

After an emotional Monday night win against the New England Patriots, the Saints traveled to FedEx Field in Landover, Maryland for a Week 13 matchup against the Washington Redskins. In the 1st quarter, the Redskins scored first with Jason Campbell throwing an 8-yard touchdown to Fred Davis. Shaun Suisham then kicked a 32-yard field goal to go up 10–0. In the 2nd quarter, the Saints finally scored with a Garrett Hartley 34-yard field goal. After a defensive stance, Drew Brees threw a 40-yard touchdown to Marques Colston which tied the game 10–10. The Redskins retook the lead with Jason Campbell connecting with Devin Thomas for a 10-yard touchdown. With the Saints now down 17–10, Brees and the Saints attempted to drive the field. Brees' pass attempt to Jeremy Shockey was intercepted by Kareem Moore. Robert Meachem then ran into Moore, stripped the football, and returned it for a 44-yard touchdown.

In the 3rd quarter, the Redskins kicker Suisham made a 28-yard field goal. The Redskins then extended their lead with Devin Thomas catching a 13-yard touchdown pass from Campbell. The Saints' Hartley made a 27-yard field goal. In the 4th quarter, Shaun Suisham and Garrett Hartley traded field goals. After an ill-advised field goal miss from 23 yards by Shaun Suisham, the Saints, only down by 7 points, now had the opportunity to tie the game. Drew Brees and the Saints offense drove the field in 5 plays, in 33 seconds and capped the drive with a 53-yard touchdown pass to Robert Meachem to tie the game 30–30 at the end of regulation. The Saints completed the comeback with Garrett Hartley's 18-yard field goal for the first lead in the game and the win 33–30 in overtime.

With the win, the Saints improved to 12–0 and clinched the NFC South title. Their 12 wins also tied a single-season franchise record set in the 1987 and 1992 seasons.

Week 14: at Atlanta Falcons

After a tough road win in overtime against the Redskins. The Saints marched into Atlanta with their eyes on a franchise best 13th straight victory. In the first quarter, Atlanta started out fast driving down the field for a Matt Bryant 36 yard field goal. The Saints responded with a Garrett Hartley 33 yard field goal. Atlanta responded with another Matt Bryant 30 yard field goal to take 6–3 lead at the end of the first quarter. The Saints would come out strong in the second quarter, when RB Reggie Bush scored on a 6 yard pass from Drew Brees to take a 10–6 lead. The Saints continued to move the ball and added on to the lead with a Marques Colston 3 yard touchdown catch from Drew Brees. Garrett Hartley kick failed giving the Saints a 16–6 lead in the second quarter. The Falcons troubles would continue. After failing to score a touchdown for the third time in the first half, Atlanta settled for a Matt Bryant 27 yard field goal to get within a touchdown at halftime.

The second half looked promising for the Saints but RB Reggie Bush fumbled and recovered the ball. RB Reggie Bush would redeem his performance on the next play with a 21 yard screen pass from Drew Brees to put the Saint up 23–9. Atlanta would make a run and wear down the Saints defense when Michael Jenkins caught a 50 yard touchdown pass from Chris Redman to move within a touchdown. Jason Snelling would add a 4 yard touchdown run to tie the game at 23. Late in the fourth quarter, the Saints would have a chance to get the lead back with a Garrett Hartley 38 yard field goal. The Saints got a break when Jonathan Vilma intercepted a Chris Redman pass to give the Saints a chance to increase the lead. The Saints would move the ball but only settle for a fake field goal that failed. The results continued in doubt for the Saints until Vilma came up with another defensive fourth-down hit on RB Jason Snelling. Stopping him a yard short of the marker with just over a minute remaining, the Saints' defense came up big but gave up 392 yards. Drew Brees threw for 296 yards for the season and threw for more than 30,000 yards in his career.He also added three touchdowns for the season and tied a club record with 120 in his Saints career. RB Reggie Bush had 47 rushing yards, 33 receiving yards and two touchdowns added for the season.

The Saints won 26–23. With the win, they improved to 13–0, clinching a first-round bye in the playoffs.

Week 15: vs. Dallas Cowboys

Coming off yet another close win, this time over the Falcons, the Saints went home for a Week 15 Saturday night duel with the Dallas Cowboys. In the first quarter, Dallas would get off to a fast start with quarterback Tony Romo completing a 49-yard TD pass to wide receiver Miles Austin. The Cowboys then increased their lead later in the quarter with a 3-yard TD run by running back Marion Barber. In the second quarter, the Saints would score their only points of the half with kicker Garrett Hartley nailing a 34-yard field goal. However, the Cowboys took a 17–3 lead at halftime with kicker Nick Folk's 44-yard field goal.

In the third quarter, Dallas scored the period's only points when running back Marion Barber got a 2-yard TD run. An exciting fourth quarter ensued. New Orleans got the first score of the period when running back Mike Bell scored from one yard out to make a 24–10 Dallas lead. Following a Dallas three-and-out, New Orleans made it a one touchdown game when quarterback Drew Brees hit wide receiver Lance Moore for a 7-yard TD pass. Dallas then marched down the field to the Saints' eight-yard line, but then kicker Nick Folk's potential game-winning 24-yard field goal hit the right goalpost and went no good, setting up another fourth quarter comeback for the Saints. However, unlike in such games against Washington and Atlanta, quarterback Drew Brees was sacked with 10 seconds left in the contest at the Dallas 48-yard line, forcing a fumble for the second time in the game by Dallas' DeMarcus Ware, which was then recovered by nose tackle Jay Ratliff. The Cowboys then took a knee to end the game.

With the loss, the Saints fell to 13–1, ending their chance at a perfect season.

Week 16: vs. Tampa Bay Buccaneers

The Saints dominated the first quarter and entered halftime riding on a 17–3 lead. Tampa Bay scored two touchdowns in the fourth quarter, including a 77-yard kick return by Micheal Spurlock, to tie the game at 17. As time expired, Garrett Hartley attempted a 37 yard field goal that would have salvaged the game for the Saints, but the kick hooked left. In overtime, Tampa Bay won the coin toss, received the kickoff, and drove down the field to win the game with a field goal, for a final score of 20–17.

With the disappointing loss, the Saints fell to 13–2, and appeared to be at risk of losing homefield advantage in the playoffs to the Vikings. However, the Vikings lost in overtime to the Chicago Bears in Week 16's Monday night game, and the Saints clinched the top seed in the NFC.

Week 17: at Carolina Panthers

After a disappointing loss to the Tampa Bay Buccaneers, the New Orleans Saints looked to rest their starters for the remaining game against the Carolina Panthers. In the First Quarter, the Carolina Panthers started out with great runs from Jonathan Stewart who capped off the first drive with a 67 yard run for a touchdown. In the second quarter the Saints got on the board with a Garrett Hartley 35 yard field goal making the score 7–3. Carolina was not done, they continued to go to their play makers like

Dwayne Jarrett who caught a 30 yard pass from Matt Moore to go up 14–3. Later John Kasay added a 41 yard field goal to extend the lead to 17–3. In the second half, the Saints could not stop Carolina from scoring twice more on a John Kasay 39 yard field goal and a 37 yard field goal to go up 23–3. The Saints would show promise when Lynell Hamilton ran for a 1 yard touchdown to end the game at 23–10.

Game Notes: Mark Brunell was dismal completing 15 of his 29 attempts for 102 yards, 1 interception and a passer rating of 45.5. This marks the first time this season that the Saints did not have a productive quarterback, receiver or running back. This marks the second time the Saints have allowed a Carolina running back to run for over 100 yards in a game (DeAngelo Williams 149 yards week 9 & Jonathan Stewart 128 yards week 17). Sitting out allowed Drew Brees to break the NFL record for completion percentage in a season with 70.60, beating the previous NFL record of 70.55 by Ken Anderson of Cincinnati set in 1982. The Saints have home-field throughout the national football conference playoffs.

Postseason

Schedule

Week	Date	Kickoff	Opponent	Results		Game Site	TV	Recap
				Final score	Team record			
WC	*First-round bye*							
DIV	January 16	3:30 PM CST	Arizona Cardinals	45–14	1–0	Louisiana Superdome	FOX	Recap [20]
CONF	January 24	5:40 PM CST	Minnesota Vikings	31–28 (OT)	2–0	Louisiana Superdome	FOX	Recap [21]
SB XLIV	February 7	5:30 PM CST	vs Indianapolis Colts	31–17	3–0	Sun Life Stadium	CBS	Recap [22]

Game summaries

NFC Wildcard Round: Bye week

By earning the NFC top-seed, the Saints earned a bye week in the first round of the NFC Playoffs.

NFC Divisonal Round: vs. Arizona Cardinals

Entering the postseason as the NFC's #1 seed, the Saints began their playoff run at home in the NFC Divisional Round against the #4 Arizona Cardinals. New Orleans would immediately trail in the first quarter as Cardinals running back Tim Hightower ran for a 70-yard touchdown. The Saints would greatly respond with a 1-yard touchdown run from running back Lynell Hamilton, quarterback Drew Brees finding tight end Jeremy Shockey on a 17-yard touchdown pass, and running back Reggie Bush's 54-yard touchdown run. Arizona would reply in the second quarter with a 4-yard touchdown run from running back Chris "Beanie" Wells. Afterwards, New Orleans struck again as Brees found wide receiver Devery Henderson on a 44-yard touchdown pass, followed by wide receiver Marques Colston for a 2-yard touchdown pass.

In the third quarter, the Saints continued their offensive day as kicker Garrett Hartley kicked a 43-yard field goal, followed by Bush's 83-yard punt return for a touchdown. For the rest of the game, New Orleans' defense took control and shut down the Cardinal's offense.

With the win, the Saints advanced to the NFC Championship Game for the second time in franchise history.

NFC Championship Game: vs. Minnesota Vikings

Coming off their divisional home win over the Cardinals, the Saints stayed at home for the NFC Championship Game against the #2 Minnesota Vikings. New Orleans would initially trail in the first quarter as Vikings running back Adrian Peterson got a 19-yard touchdown run, yet the Saints responded with quarterback Drew Brees hooking up with running back Pierre Thomas on a 38-yard touchdown pass. However, Minnesota would answer with quarterback Brett Favre completing a 9-yard touchdown pass to wide receiver Sidney Rice. New Orleans would tie the game again in the second quarter with Brees finding wide receiver Devery Henderson on a 9-yard touchdown pass.

The Saints would take the lead in the third quarter with Thomas' 9-yard touchdown run, but the Vikings would tie the game with a 1-yard touchdown run from Peterson. In the fourth quarter, New Orleans would regain the lead as Brees found running back Reggie Bush on a 5-yard touchdown pass, yet Minnesota would tie again with Peterson's 2-yard touchdown run. A key interception late in 4th quarter by Tracy Porter stopped what could have been Minnesota's game winning drive, leading to overtime. In overtime, the Saints came out on top as kicker Garrett Hartley booted the game-winning 40-yard field goal.

With the win, not only did the Saints improve their overall record to 15–3, but they would advance to their very first Super Bowl in franchise history.

Super Bowl XLIV: vs. Indianapolis Colts

In continuation of a string of firsts, the Saints advanced to their first Super Bowl in franchise history and won it in dramatic fashion. After the coin toss, the Saints wanted the ball first; however, this didn't help their first drive. The Colts drove the ball down the field with an attempt to score the first touchdown but was denied and forced Matt Stover to kick a 38 yard goal. But the Colts were not finished: on their next possession, Pierre Garcon caught a 19 yard TD pass from Peyton Manning, and the Colts led 10–0 after fifteen minutes. In the second quarter, the Saints were forced to look upon Garrett Hartley for two field goals – a 46 yarder and a 44 yarder respectively – and the deficit was reduced to four points by halftime.

Kicking off the second half, the Saints caught Indy by surprise with the "Ambush" play (an onside kick in kickoff formation), which the Saints recovered, shifting the momentum to them. Pierre Thomas caught a 16 yard screen pass from Drew Brees and NO had their first lead of the game, 13–10 after the extra point. The Colts would not be denied from scoring again with the rushing attack of Joseph Addai, capping off the scoring drive with a 4-yard run. From here, however, the Colts would be denied. The Saints still stood by Hartley to keep the game close with a 47 yard field goal, taking the score to 17–16. In the fourth quarter, Jeremy Shockey caught a two-yard touchdown pass from Drew Brees with Lance Moore catching a two-point conversion and the Saints led 24–17. In the end, it was the defense that came through when Tracy Porter intercepted and returned 74 yards for a touchdown to seal the win and the first Super Bowl title for the New Orleans Saints in their 44 year existence.

External links

- 2009 New Orleans Saints season at Pro Football Reference [23]
- 2009 New Orleans Saints season at ESPN [24]

2010 New Orleans Saints season

The 2010 New Orleans Saints season will be the 44th for the franchise in the National Football League (NFL) and city of New Orleans, Louisiana, and will be the 33rd to host home games in the Louisiana Superdome. The Saints enter their new season for the first time as defending Super Bowl and National Football Conference (NFC) champions, and will play in the NFC South Division. The franchise will attempt to act upon their most successful season in franchise history from 2009, which they began undefeated for 13 consecutive games only to lose their last three games at the end of the season to finish 13–3. In addition, they will also attempt to win the NFC South Division title for the third time in history, earn a first-ever second consecutive playoff berth since 1991, and successfully defend their conference and league championships. For Sean Payton, this will be his fifth year as head coach for the Saints; he has compiled a team record of 38–26 in regular season and 4–1 in post-season.

Offseason

2010 NFL Draft

As the winners of Super Bowl XLIV, the Saints are scheduled to acquire the 32nd pick in the first round and are scheduled to generally draft in this order.

New Orleans Saints 2010 NFL Draft selections

Draft order			Player name	Position	Height	Weight	College	Contract	Notes
Round	Choice	Overall							
1	32	32	Patrick Robinson	CB					
2	32	64	Charles Brown	OT					
3	31	95	Jimmy Graham	TE					
4	25	123	Al Woods	DT					
5	27	158	Matt Tennant	C					
6	32	TBD	*Traded to the Arizona Cardinals*						
7	32	239	Sean Canfield	QB					

Roster signings

All signings were to active roster, except where otherwise noted.

Pos.	Player	Date	Notes
CB	Greg Fassitt	February 12, 2010	
TE	Tyler Lorenzen	February 12, 2010	
T	Jermey Parnell	February 12, 2010	
WR	Matt Simon	February 12, 2010	
G	Na'Shan Goddard	February 18, 2010	
CB	Glenn Sharpe	February 18, 2010	
DT	Earl Heyman	February 18, 2010	
G	Tim Duckworth	February 19, 2010	
RB	Zak Keasey	February 23, 2010	
DE	Alex Brown	April 7, 2010	
DE	Jimmy Wilkerson	April 20, 2010	
LB	Clint Ingram	May 19, 2010	

Roster releases

Pos.	Player	Date	Notes
WR	D'Juan Woods	February 16, 2010	Released after being placed on injured reserve prior to the 2009 season
OL	Jamar Nesbit	March 4, 2010	
LB	Mark Simoneau	March 4, 2010	
DL	Charles Grant	March 5, 2010	
G	Jamar Nesbit	March 5, 2010	

Schedule

Preseason

The Saints preseason schedule was announced on March 31, 2010.

Week	Date	Kickoff	Opponent	Results		Site	TV	NFL.com Recap
				Final Score	Team Record			
1	August 12	6:30 p.m. CDT	at New England Patriots			Gillette Stadium	CST	
2	August 21	7:00 p.m. CDT	Houston Texans			Louisiana Superdome	CST	
3	August 27	7:00 p.m. CDT	San Diego Chargers			Louisiana Superdome	CBS	
4	September 2	7:00 p.m. CDT	at Tennessee Titans			LP Field	CST	

Regular season

Listed below are the Saints' opponents for 2010. As the defending Super Bowl champions, the Saints will host the annual NFL Kickoff Game on Thursday, September 9, against the Minnesota Vikings, which results in a rematch of the 2009 NFC Championship Game. The pregame concert and game will be televised on NBC.

The remainder of the Saints' schedule was announced on April 20, 2010.

Week	Date	Kickoff	Opponent	Results		Site	TV	NFL.com Recap
				Final Score	Team Record			
1	September 9	7:30 p.m. CDT	Minnesota Vikings			Louisiana Superdome	NBC	
2	September 20	7:30 p.m. CDT	at San Francisco 49ers			Candlestick Park	ESPN	
3	September 26	12:00 p.m. CDT	Atlanta Falcons			Louisiana Superdome	Fox	
4	October 3	12:00 p.m. CDT	Carolina Panthers			Louisiana Superdome	Fox	
5	October 10	3:05 p.m. CDT	at Arizona Cardinals			University of Phoenix Stadium	Fox	

6	October 17	12:00 p.m. CDT	at Tampa Bay Buccaneers			Raymond James Stadium	Fox	
7	October 24	12:00 p.m. CDT	Cleveland Browns			Louisiana Superdome	CBS	
8	October 31	7:20 p.m. CDT	Pittsburgh Steelers			Louisiana Superdome	NBC	
9	November 7	12:00 p.m. CST	at Carolina Panthers			Bank of America Stadium	Fox	
10	Bye							
11	November 21	3:05 p.m. CST*	Seattle Seahawks			Louisiana Superdome	Fox	
12	November 25	3:15 p.m. CST	at Dallas Cowboys			Cowboys Stadium	Fox	
13	December 5	12:00 p.m. CST*	at Cincinnati Bengals			Paul Brown Stadium	Fox	
14	December 12	3:05 p.m. CST*	St. Louis Rams			Louisiana Superdome	Fox	
15	December 19	12:00 p.m. CST*	at Baltimore Ravens			M&T Bank Stadium	Fox	
16	December 27	7:30 p.m. CST	at Atlanta Falcons			Georgia Dome	ESPN	
17	January 2	12:00 p.m. CST*	Tampa Bay Buccaneers			Louisiana Superdome	Fox	

Indicates that the game time is subject to change as a result of flexible scheduling.

Personnel

External links

- New Orleans Saints official website [1]
- New Orleans Saints NFL.com profile [1]

Super Bowl XLIV

Super Bowl XLIV

Super Bowl XLIV was an American football game between the American Football Conference (AFC) champion Indianapolis Colts and the National Football Conference (NFC) champion New Orleans Saints to decide the National Football League (NFL) champion for the 2009 season. The Saints (16-3) defeated the Colts (16-3) by a score of 31–17, earning their first Super Bowl win. New Orleans quarterback Drew Brees, who completed 32 of 39 passes for 288 yards and two touchdowns, was named the Super Bowl MVP. His 32 completions tied a Super Bowl record set by Tom Brady in Super Bowl XXXVIII. With the victory, the Saints became the fourth team to win in their only Super Bowl appearance after the New York Jets, Baltimore Ravens and Tampa Bay Buccaneers.

The game was played at Sun Life Stadium in Miami Gardens, Florida on February 7, 2010 for the fifth time (and in South Florida for the tenth time), the latest calendar date for a Super Bowl yet. The game was the Saints' first Super Bowl appearance and the fourth for the Colts franchise. All four of the Colts' Super Bowl games have been played in Miami, with their first two games in the former Miami Orange Bowl and the last two in the current Miami stadium (which has changed names several times since its opening, most recently in January 2010).

The Saints entered the game with a 13–3 record for the 2009 regular season, compared to the Colts' 14–2 record. In the playoff games, both teams placed first in their respective conferences. It was the first time since Super Bowl XXVIII (16 years previously) that both number one seeds have reached the Super Bowl. The Colts entered the Super Bowl off of 20–3 and 30–17 victories (over the Baltimore Ravens and New York Jets, respectively), while the Saints advanced with scores of 45–14 and 31–28 (in overtime), defeating last year's runners up the Arizona Cardinals in their first game and the Minnesota Vikings in the second. The Pittsburgh Steelers, as defending champions, failed to make the playoffs based on tiebreakers. The Saints' head coach was Sean Payton, having joined from the Dallas Cowboys in 2006, while opposing head coach Jim Caldwell was appointed the Colts' head coach in 2009, having joined them in 2002 as assistant head coach.

It was the tenth time the Super Bowl has been held in Miami at the home stadium of the Miami Dolphins: the now-Sun Life Stadium had hosted four previous Super Bowls (XXIII, XXIX, XXXIII, and XLI) and five were played in the Dolphins' now demolished former home, the Miami Orange Bowl (II, III, V, X, XIII). The game was broadcast live on CBS, with the National Anthem sung by Carrie Underwood and the halftime show that featured the British rock band The Who.

Per convention as an even numbered Super Bowl, the Colts, as the AFC representatives, had the home team designation, wearing blue jerseys with white pants, while the Saints (who wore their white jerseys in several home games this year) wore white jerseys with gold pants. The Saints' victory extended the white jersey winning streak to six, dating back to Super Bowl XXXIX, while the Colts dropped to 0–2 all-time wearing their blue jerseys, the other loss being their loss to the New York Jets in Super Bowl III.

Background

Host selection process

The league initially voted on March 23, 2005, that New York City host the game, contingent on the completion of the proposed West Side Stadium being built for the New York Jets by 2008. After New York state government officials declined to approve $400 million for the stadium, the NFL decided to reopen the bidding for the game's site. The league reconsidered the other, unsuccessful candidates for Super Bowl XLIII: Atlanta, Houston, and Miami. On October 6, 2008, the league selected Miami as the host city.

With Tampa as the host of Super Bowl XLIII, Super Bowl XLIV marked the third time that consecutive Super Bowls have been played in the same state. Super Bowls II and III were both played at the Orange Bowl. Super Bowls XXI and XXII were both played in California: XXI at Pasadena's Rose Bowl Stadium and XXII at San Diego's Jack Murphy Stadium.

Miami became the first city to host two Super Bowls designated as a National Special Security Event (NSSE). In the wake of the September 11, 2001 terrorist attacks, every Super Bowl since Super Bowl XXXVI has been designated as an NSSE. Super Bowl XLI was Miami's first Super Bowl designated as an NSSE.

Pro Bowl changes

The 2010 Pro Bowl was played on January 31, during the off-week between the conference championships and the Super Bowl, breaking with the precedent of scheduling the game for the Sunday after the Super Bowl. The game also changed venues from Aloha Stadium in Honolulu, Hawaii, where it had been held since 1979, to Sun Life Stadium in Miami (the same city and stadium hosting the Super Bowl itself). A total of 14 players from the Super Bowl participants – seven each from the Colts and the Saints – did not play in the Pro Bowl. The new schedule took advantage of the bye week given to the conference champions to rest and prepare for the Super Bowl. The NFL has indicated this may not be a permanent transition, and has discussed a possible rotating location for the Pro Bowl in the future. The game will return to Hawaii in 2011 and 2012, however.

The move also meant that the Pro Bowl, which was won by the AFC by a score of 41–34, would avoid competing against the 2010 NBA All-Star Game, the second full day of competition in the 2010 Winter

Olympics, and the 52nd running of the Daytona 500, as would have been the case had the game been played on February 14 per its traditional post-Super Bowl scheduling.

Teams

New Orleans Saints

The New Orleans Saints finished the season with an NFC best 13–3 record and went on to advance to the first Super Bowl in their 43 years as an NFL team. After joining the NFL in 1967, it took them 21 years to record their first winning season and another 13 years after that to win their first playoff game. Five years later, the New Orleans area suffered another setback when the Louisiana Superdome was devastated with the rest of the city by Hurricane Katrina, forcing them to play all of their home games in elsewhere as they finished with a 3–13 record (see *Effect of Hurricane Katrina on the New Orleans Saints*). But in the offseason, the team's fortunes began to turn. First, they signed pro bowl quarterback Drew Brees, who would go on to throw for more passing yards than any other quarterback over the next four seasons. They also drafted multi-talented Heisman Trophy winning running back Reggie Bush, receiver Marques Colston, and guard Jahri Evans, three players who would become major contributors on the Saints' offense. The following season, New Orleans improved to 10–6 and advanced to the NFC title game for the first time, which they lost to the Chicago Bears. Although they failed to make the playoffs over the next two seasons, they continued to sign new talent, and by 2009 they were ready to make another run at the Super Bowl.

The Saints' offense led the NFL in scoring, averaging just under 32 points per game. Brees finished the season as the NFL's top rated quarterback (109.6), completing an NFL-record 70.6% of his passes for 4,338 yards and 34 touchdowns, with just 11 interceptions. His top target was Colston, who caught 70 passes for 1,074 yards and 9 touchdowns, but he had plenty of other weapons, such as receivers Devery Henderson (51 receptions) and Robert Meachem (45), along with tight ends Jeremy Shockey (48) and Dave Thomas (35). The ground attack was led by running backs Pierre Thomas and Mike Bell. Thomas rushed for 793 yards and caught 39 passes for 302, while Bell added 654 yards on the ground. Bush was also a major contributor, rushing for 390 yards (with a 5.6 yards per carry average), catching 47 passes for 335 yards, and adding another 130 yards returning punts. New Orleans also had a strong offensive line with three Pro Bowl selections: guard Jahri Evans, center Jonathan Goodwin, and tackle Jon Stinchcomb

Defensive lineman Will Smith led the team in sacks with 13. Another big weapon on defense was linebacker Jonathan Vilma, who led the team with 87 tackles and intercepted three passes. The Saints' secondary was led by 12-year veteran safety Darren Sharper, who recorded 9 interceptions and set an NFL record by returning them for 376 yards and three touchdowns. Cornerback Tracy Porter was also effective, recording 49 tackles and 4 picks with one touchdown.

Like the Colts, the Saints also started out the season strong, winning their first 13 games. But then they became the first 13–0 team ever to lose their last three games of the year. After losing their next game to the Dallas Cowboys 24–17, they suffered a narrow loss to the Tampa Bay Buccaneers in overtime after Garrett Hartley missed a potential game winning field goal, and then closed out the season with a 23–10 loss to the Carolina Panthers. Still, they clinched the #1 NFC playoff seed and scored 76 points in their two playoff wins en route to their first ever Super Bowl.

Indianapolis Colts

Indianapolis had the NFL best 14–2 record, winning seven games by less than a touchdown , on their way to earning their second Super Bowl appearance in the last four years. Once again, the Colts boasted a powerful offense led by 10-time Pro Bowl quarterback Peyton Manning, who threw for 4,500 yards and 33 touchdowns during the season, with only 16 interceptions, earning him a 99.9 passer rating and a league record fourth National Football League Most Valuable Player Award. Under the protection of pro bowl center Jeff Saturday and the rest of the line, Manning had been sacked just 13 times during the regular season, the fewest in the NFL. His top targets were veteran receiver Reggie Wayne and tight end Dallas Clark, who both recorded 100 receptions and 10 touchdowns. Wayne led the team with 1,260 yards, while Clark was second with 1,106. Manning also had other reliable targets, such as recently acquired receivers Austin Collie (60 receptions for 676 yards and 7 touchdowns) and Pierre Garçon (47 receptions for 765 yards and 4 touchdowns). Running back Joseph Addai led the Colts' ground game with 821 rushing yards and 10 touchdowns, while also catching 51 passes for another 336 yards and 3 scores.

Indianapolis's defensive line was led by Pro Bowl defensive ends Robert Mathis and Dwight Freeney. Freeney led the team with 13.5 sacks, while Mathis added 9.5 sacks and forced 5 fumbles. Behind them, the Colts had a solid corps of linebackers featuring Clint Session and Gary Brackett, who each recorded 80 tackles. Pro bowl safety Antoine Bethea led the secondary with 70 tackles and four interceptions.

Under their new coach Jim Caldwell, the Colts started off the season with 14 consecutive wins before suffering their first loss to the New York Jets, 29–15, a game in which Caldwell made the controversial decision to rest his starters after the team took a slim lead rather than keep them in to play for a chance at a 16–0 season. Indianapolis finished the season at 14–2 following a loss to the Buffalo Bills, in which they rested their starters and went on to advance to the Super Bowl, making them perfect in all their games in which their starters played all four quarters.

Caldwell led the Colts to the Super Bowl the season after Tony Dungy retired, just like in Tampa Bay when Jon Gruden led the Bucs to Super Bowl XXXVII after Dungy was fired. Senior offensive line coach Howard Mudd retired following the game.

Playoffs

Indianapolis's first opponent was the Baltimore Ravens, a 9–7 squad that had advanced to the divisional round by blowing out the New England Patriots 33–14, forcing four turnovers from their all-pro quarterback Tom Brady. Against the Colts however, all they could manage was a field goal on their opening drive. Indianapolis built up a 17–3 first half lead with a Matt Stover field goal and Manning's touchdown passes to Wayne and Collie. In the second half, the Colts survived two interceptions from Baltimore safety Ed Reed on one drive, one of which Reed fumbled, and the other which was called back by a penalty. Stover, who spent 18 years with the Modell franchise, finished the drive with his second field goal to make final score 20–3, as their defense put the game away by forcing two consecutive turnovers.

Their next opponent was the Jets, who had made the playoffs in part due to Caldwell's decision to bench his starters in their Week 16 meeting. This time, the Colts would have to mount a comeback, as New York built up a 17–6 first half lead. Yet Indianapolis would step up to the challenge, scoring 24 unanswered points. First, Manning completed three passes to Collie for 80 yards, the last one a 16-yard touchdown completion to cut the score to 17–13 at the end of the half. Manning added two more touchdown passes in the second half, one to Garçon and one to Clark, and Stover added a 21-yard field goal to close out the scoring. Manning finished the game with 377 passing yards and three touchdowns, while Garçon and Collie had over 100 receiving yards each.

Meanwhile, New Orleans started off their playoff run with a dominating 45–14 win over the defending NFC champion Arizona Cardinals. Arizona was coming off a 51–45 overtime win over the Green Bay Packers in which they racked up 531 yards against a defense ranked second in the league in total yards allowed. However, although Arizona scored on their first play of the game, New Orleans dominated the Cardinals with 35 points in the first half. First, Lynell Hamilton scored on a 1-yard run. Then, Sharper recovered a fumble from Arizona, setting up Brees' touchdown pass to Shockey. Following a punt, Bush scored on a franchise playoff record 46-yard run. In the second quarter, Brees added two more touchdown passes, one to Henderson on a flea flicker and the other to Colston that was set up by a Will Smith interception, giving them a 35–14 first half lead before adding 10 more points in the second half on a Hartley field goal and Bush's 83-yard punt return. Bush racked up 217 all-purpose yards, while Brees threw for 247 yards and three touchdowns.

Their opponent in the NFC championship game was the Minnesota Vikings, led by 11-time pro bowl quarterback Brett Favre, who had thrown four touchdown passes in their divisional round win over the Dallas Cowboys. Even though the Saints' offense could only muster 257 total yards, their defense made up for it by forcing five turnovers. Additionally, the Saints outgained the Vikings in punt and kickoff return yards 166 to 50. The key play of the game occurred late in the fourth quarter with the score tied 28–28 and the Vikings driving for a potential game-winning field goal. With less than a minute left, they reached the Saints 33-yard line. But after two runs for no gain and a penalty that pushed them back to the 38, Porter picked off a pass from Favre to send the game into overtime. After New Orleans won the coin toss, Pierre Thomas' 40-yard kickoff return set up a 10-play, 39-yard drive that ended with a game winning 40-yard field goal by Hartley, sending the Saints to their first ever Super Bowl.

This is the first Super Bowl matchup in which both teams had a first-round bye since Super Bowl XXXIX. All four of the Super Bowls in between had one team that played all three rounds (two of which were wild-card teams), with three of those teams (including the Colts in Super Bowl XLI) winning it all.

Broadcasting

Television

United States

The game was televised live in the United States on CBS, capping the network's 50th season of NFL coverage (1956–93; 1998–present). This was the 17th Super Bowl telecast for CBS, the largest total among the "big four" US television networks. CBS had also broadcast the previous Super Bowl held in South Florida (XLI). Play-by-play announcer Jim Nantz and color commentator Phil Simms were in the broadcast booth, with Steve Tasker and Solomon Wilcots serving as sideline reporters. The game was preceded by *The Super Bowl Today*, a four-hour pregame show that was hosted by James Brown and started at 2 pm US EST. A kickoff show for the game aired from 6 pm US EST to 6:28 pm US EST.

With an average US audience of 106.5 million viewers, this was the most-watched Super Bowl ever as well as the most-watched program of any kind in American television history, beating the 27-year-long record previously held by the final episode of *M*A*S*H*, "Goodbye, Farewell and Amen", watched by 105.97 million viewers. An estimated 153.4 million total viewers watched all or part of the game. The game drew a national Nielsen rating of 45.0 with a 68 share, the highest for a Super Bowl since Super Bowl XXX in 1996 (46.0/68). The telecast drew a 56.3 rating in New Orleans and a 54.2 rating in Indianapolis, first and fourth respectively among local markets.

Commercials

Notable returnees and absences

Perennial Super Bowl advertisers Anheuser–Busch InBev and CareerBuilder stated their commitment to advertise in Super Bowl XLIV, showing eight and two different spots during the game, respectively. A 30-second spot cost US $2.8 million with several advertisers getting discounts, down from last year's $3 million. All advertising slots were sold out on February 1, 2010, six days before the game. Pepsi-Cola had previously stated their commitment to advertise, but then said they would not be buying any commercial time, marking the first time in 23 years that Pepsi did not run an ad during the Super Bowl itself. FedEx also stated that they would not buy ad time. Both Pepsi and FedEx are official NFL sponsors. Coca-Cola and Dr Pepper Snapple Group capitalized on Pepsi's absence by buying ads in the game; Dr Pepper's ad featured KISS performing "Calling Dr. Love," while one of Coca-Cola's three ads featured Montgomery Burns (of *The Simpsons*) losing everything he owns. Also for the second straight year, one of the Big Three American automobile makers — General Motors — did not have a commercial in the game. Ford had one commercial for the Ford Edge featuring Mike Rowe. Chrysler's Dodge brand did advertise this year for its Dodge Charger, narrated by Michael C. Hall.

What aired

Frito-Lay's Doritos brand, in turn owned by PepsiCo, had four consumer-created advertisements scheduled. The first three ads – running in the first quarter – featured a sly dog using an anti-bark collar to his advantage to steal a man's Doritos, a fast-handed boy defending his Doritos and his mother from a potential suitor, and a man faking his death for free Doritos. The fourth ad, featuring an angry gym rat who was overprotective for his Doritos being stolen, aired in the fourth quarter. Had three of the ads topped the USA Today Super Bowl Ad Meter rankings, the commercial's creators would have won a total of US $5 million ($1 million for first, $600,000 for second and $400,000 for third, plus a $1 million bonus for each of the three finalists). The previous year, Joe and David Herbert's "Free Doritos" ad topped the survey and won $1 million. The United States Census Bureau spent $2.5 million on a 30-second spot, directed by noted independent filmmaker Christopher Guest, for the 2010 United States Census, which urged Americans to answer its questionnaires that will be sent out in the next few weeks. McDonald's aired a commercial, updating a famous ad from the early 1990s, in which NBA superstars LeBron James and Dwight Howard (replacing Michael Jordan and Larry Bird) play an otherworldly game of H-O-R-S-E, with a McDonald's lunch going to the winner - however, they soon look over and see that Bird has helped himself to it. Mars Chocolate returned three years after its controversial Snickers ad that was protested by gay groups with two men kissing one another that was pulled one day following the game (see *Super Bowl XLI: Commercials*). The commercial – winner of the annual Ad Meter survey – featured veteran actors Betty White and Abe Vigoda playing full-contact backyard football.

The rest of the Top Five:

2. The aforementioned Doritos' amateur ad featuring a dog strapped to a anti-bark collar getting revenge on a teasing man.

3. A Bud Light ad with a house completely made of beer cans of the sponsor's product.

4. A Budweiser ad featuring the relationship between a Clydesdale and a Longhorn steer.

5. Coca Cola's man walking through an African savanna in the middle of the night.

The YouTube Top Five of their "2010 Ad Blitz" were:

1. Another Doritos ad that showed a kid slapping his mom's suitor.

2. Etrade's baby with his girlfriend.

3. The Doritos dog collar ad.

4. The Snickers Betty White/Abe Vigoda ad.

5. The Doritos commercial with the gym rat.

Internet domain registrar GoDaddy, which created a racy ad the year after the Super Bowl XXXVIII halftime show controversy, bought two ads in the Super Bowl for the sixth consecutive year. Advertising Age reported that Paramount Pictures bought a Super Bowl spot for the upcoming films *Iron Man 2* and *The Last Airbender*. A trailer for the HBO miniseries *The Pacific* was also aired.

Other advertisers for 2010 included Homeaway Inc.,,, paying tribute to *National Lampoon's Vacation* with their stars Chevy Chase and Beverly D'Angelo, and Diamond Foods, who returned to promote both its Emerald Nuts brand and Pop Secret popcorn, which they bought from General Mills two years before. Boost Mobile aired a special ad, celebrating the 25th Anniversary of The Super Bowl Shuffle, featuring many of the 1985 Chicago Bears to advertise their US $50 per month service. Also, in a CBS-produced promo for the *Late Show with David Letterman*, the eponymous host and his longtime talk show rival, Jay Leno, appeared together with Oprah Winfrey.

Controversies

Three advertisers in particular raised eyebrows with their choice to advertise during the Super Bowl. One new advertiser, Focus on the Family, aired a commercial featuring 2007 Heisman Trophy winner Tim Tebow and his mother that elicited criticism from some women's groups who demanded CBS cancel the ad because they claimed it would be divisive, under the impression that it would mention Tebow's mother was advised, for health issues, to abort her son Tim, but she chose to give birth to him. In the first quarter, CBS aired the advertisement, which had not been pre-released to the public. Per a statement released earlier, the ad did not mention the topic of abortion explicitly.

One proposed sponsor, ManCrunch, a gay dating site that bills itself as a place "where many many many men come out to play," had expressed interest in purchasing a 30-second advertisement. The ManCrunch advertisement would have depicted a male Green Bay Packers fan and a male Minnesota Vikings fan reaching into the same bowl of potato chips at the same time and, after a brief pause, begin to passionately kiss. ManCrunch's ad, which has since been released to the public, was initially put on a waiting list before the network outright rejected it due to it violating CBS's broadcast standards. ManCrunch immediately accused CBS of discrimination. Some observers suspect that their advertisement was an attempt at ambush marketing and free publicity. Another ad that was rejected by CBS for failure to meet standards was for the texting service kgb, which focuses on two men with CGI-enhanced images bent over with their heads in their posteriors, while an actor, Sean Gunn, portraying an agent stated that "They had their head up their [backsides]". kgb instead aired an ad with two people who had to find the Japanese word for "I surrender" before being run over by a sumo wrestler. Another ad for Bud Light which was rejected showed workers stripping down for a charity clothes drive in exchange for free beer. All of the rejected ads were shown on YouTube.

Among other rejected or modified ads were one for Electronic Arts' *Dante's Inferno*, which had to be edited for content (the closing phrase, originally intended to read "go to Hell," was replaced with "Hell awaits"), and GoDaddy's originally planned advertisement. Career Builder's ad, showing people dressed too casually for "Casual Friday" and a Dockers ad to promote a free pair of their pants with men in shirts but sans trousers aired back-to-back early in the second quarter.

An E*TRADE advertisement, continuing their theme of talking babies on a Web cam, featured a boyfriend-stealing, "milkaholic" baby girl named "Lindsay." Actress Lindsay Lohan, who has a history of alcoholism and was noted for having tried in the early 2000s to date popular young men who were already dating other women, is suing E*TRADE over the advertisement and seeking US$100,000,000 in damages, under the impression that the advertisement defamed her via subliminal messaging and violated her personality rights. E*TRADE denied the allegations and stated the name "Lindsay" came from a member of the accounting staff.

International telecasts

Viewers worldwide were able to watch on the following channels:

- North America:
    - ": CTV (English) and RDS (French)
    - ": Televisa, TV Azteca (broadcasting in HD).
    - ": Tropical Vision Limited, Great Belize Television.
    - ": ESPN, Fox Sports Latin America.
- Oceania
    - ": Fox Sports 3, ESPN, Channel Ten and One HD
    - ": Sky Sport 2 and ESPN
- Europe:
    - ": Puls 4 started at 23:30 (CET)
    - ": Prime Sport
    - ": TV3+ starting at 22:00 (CET)
    - ": ESPN America.
    - ": Nelonen Sport Pro and on Viasat Sport/Viasat Sport HD started at 00:00 (CET)
    - ": W9
    - ": ARD Das Erste started at 23:35 (CET)
    - : Nova Sports started 01:30 (EET)
    - ": Sport 1
    - ": Rai Sport Più started at 22:00 (CET), Rai Due started at 00:15 (CET), broadcasted also in HD in selected areas.
    - ": NRK1 started at 23:15 (CET) and on Viasat Sport/Viasat Sport HD
    - ": Polsat Sport/Polsat Sport HD started at 00:00 (CET)

- ": SportTV 2 and on SportTV HD started at 23:00 (WET)
- ": Sport 1 started 01:00 (EET)
- ": NTV Plus
- ": Šport TV
- ": Canal+
- ": TV6 and on Viasat Sport/Viasat Sport HD started at 00:00 (CET).
- ": Turkey'''": Fox Sports [Turkey] Spormax HD started 01.00 (EET)
- ' and ': BBC One and on Sky Sports 1 and HD 1 at 10:55 pm and 11 pm (GMT)

- South America:
  - ": ESPN, Bandsports - live started at 21:00 (Brazilian Summer Time) and Rede Bandeirantes - condensed version aired at 00:30 BRST
  - ' and ': ESPN, Fox Sports Latin America
  - ": ESPN, Fox Sports Latin America, Meridiano Television
- Asia:
  - ": CCTV-5, G-Sports, Guangdong Sports, Sina TV
  - ": ATV
  - ": NHK, NTV

Radio

On radio, Westwood One had the national English-language broadcast rights to the game in the United States and Canada. Marv Albert (play-by-play) and Boomer Esiason (color commentator) called the game for the network; it was the last broadcast Albert would do for Westwood One, due to his desire to focus on his basketball coverage duties. The teams' flagship stations also carried the game with their respective local announcers: WLHK-FM and WFNI-AM in Indianapolis (with Bob Lamey and Will Wolford announcing) and WWL-FM/AM in New Orleans (with Jim Henderson and Hokie Gajan announcing). Univision Radio aired a Spanish-language feed for Hispanophone American listeners (with Clemson Smith-Muñiz and David Crommett announcing).

Sirius XM Satellite Radio carried 14 game feeds in ten languages to Sirius subscribers, as well as to XM subscribers with the "Best of Sirius" package. In addition to the four US feeds mentioned above, Sirius carried the following international feeds:

- ": BBC Radio 5 Live (English; Arlo White announcing)
- ": Canal+ Spain (Spanish)
- ": NTV Plus (Russian)
- ": W9 (French)
- ": NHK (Japanese)
- ": ARD (German)
- ": RAI (Italian)

- ": Sport1 (Hungarian)
- ": Prime Sport (Dutch)
- ": Viasat (Danish)

FieldPass, the subscription Internet radio service provided by the league at NFL.com, also carried most of these feeds. Due to contractual restrictions, only Sirius XM and FieldPass were permitted to carry the local team broadcasts along with WLHK, WFNI and WWL, with the teams' other network radio affiliates instead airing the Westwood One feed.

Entertainment and other ceremonies

Pregame

Barenaked Ladies played the Super Bowl Saturday Night event with O.A.R. and Robert Randolph & The Family Band.

The instrumental for the songs "Misguided Ghosts" and "Playing God" off Paramore's latest album Brand New Eyes played during the introduction of players and during an excerpt of Drew Brees' patronage to the city of New Orleans.

Chris Daughtry, Steve Winwood and Queen Latifah performed during the Super Bowl pre-game tailgate party, which started at 2 p.m.

Carrie Underwood sang the National Anthem and Queen Latifah sang "America the Beautiful." Underwood's selection marks the third straight year that an alumnus of *American Idol* has been chosen to perform "The Star-Spangled Banner," joining Jordin Sparks at Super Bowl XLII and Jennifer Hudson a year later. Translation of both songs into American Sign Language was provided by Kinesha Battles, a student at the Florida School for the Deaf and Blind.

The Pro Football Hall of Fame Class of 2010, led by Jerry Rice and Emmitt Smith, participated in the pre-game coin toss; Smith actually tossed the coin. The rest of the class — Rickey Jackson, Dick LeBeau, Floyd Little, Russ Grimm and John Randle — were named the day before. The Saints won the coin toss, marking the 13th straight Super Bowl the NFC won the toss (the Cardinals won the toss in Super Bowl XLIII but elected to defer to the second half, giving the Steelers the ball to open the game).

The Saints entered the Sun Life Stadium field first, to The Alan Parsons Project's "Sirius", which was made famous for team introductions by the Chicago Bulls.

The Colts entered last, as they were the "home" team, to "Won't Get Fooled Again" by The Who, which coincidentally would be performed by the band during the halftime show.

Halftime

The Who performed at the Super Bowl XLIV halftime show. The band played a medley of their hits, consisting of "Pinball Wizard", "Baba O'Riley", "Who Are You", "See Me, Feel Me", and "Won't Get Fooled Again" (three of these songs are also the themes for the *CSI* TV series, which air on CBS, just like Super Bowl XLIV did). For the first time since the Super Bowl XXXIV halftime show, there was no crowd of fans surrounding the halftime stage.

Merchandising

Retailers had ordered much more New Orleans Saints merchandise prior to the game than they had ordered Colts merchandise. The NFL estimates that US $100 million worth of Super Bowl merchandise will be sold this year.

Game summary

First quarter

The Saints won the toss and chose to receive, but their first possession resulted in a punt after going three-and-out.

The Colts offense took the field for the first time, with the ball spotted at their own 27 yard line. The Colts put together a drive that went 53 yards and resulted in a 38-yard field goal by kicker Matt Stover. At 42 years old, Stover became the oldest person in NFL history to play in a Super Bowl.

Following the game's first score, Courtney Roby returned the ensuing kickoff to the New Orleans 26 yard line. Approaching the 25-yard line, Roby swooped into a dive and appeared to fumble the ball, but he was ruled down by contact. This time, the Saints managed to get a first down with a 16-yard completion from Drew Brees to Reggie Bush, but they were eventually forced to punt again. Punter Thomas Morstead pinned the Colts back at their own 4-yard line with a 46-yard kick.

Indianapolis responded with a 96-yard scoring drive, tying the record for the longest drive in Super Bowl history. Joseph Addai rushed three times for 53 yards on the drive, while Manning completed three passes for 35 yards, the last one a 19-yard touchdown pass to Pierre Garçon, increasing the Colts lead to 10–0.

Second quarter

The Saints' next drive carried over from the previous quarter. Brees completed three passes for 36 yards as the Saints advanced to the Colts' 22-yard line. But on third down, Brees was sacked for a 7-yard loss by Dwight Freeney, forcing New Orleans to settle for a 46-yard field goal from Garrett Hartley.

In the final two minutes of the first half, the Saints drove to a 1st-and-goal at the Colts' 3 yard line. A false start penalty set them back to the 8, and after getting a yard away from the end zone, they attempted 3rd and 4th down runs. They failed to convert both times. The Colts ran three straight running plays in an effort to wind down the clock and go to halftime with a seven point lead, but the Saints kept the Colts from getting another first down. Following Bush's 4-yard punt return to the New Orleans 48, with only one timeout left to use in the half, the Saints got back into field goal territory, and Hartley hit a 44-yard field goal as time expired, with the Colts still leading 10–6. This was the first 10–6 halftime score in Super Bowl history.

Third quarter

The Colts were set to receive the ball to start the second half, but were caught by surprise when the Saints executed an onside kick. This was the first onside kick attempted before the fourth quarter in Super Bowl history, a play the Saints referred to as "Ambush." Thomas Morstead kicked the ball to his left, and after traveling almost 15 yards, the ball bounced off the facemask of the Colts' Hank Baskett, who failed to make a clean recovery. Several players dove for the loose ball, creating a pile that took over a minute for the officiating crew to separate. When the dust finally cleared, linebacker Jonathan Casillas of New Orleans was officially credited with the recovery on the 42-yard line, but Casillas and other Saints players insisted that it was actually safety Chris Reis who came up with the football. The Saints' offense took over and stormed down the field on an effective 58-yard drive in which they never faced a third down. Brees completed five consecutive passes for 58 yards on the drive and capped it off with a screen pass to Pierre Thomas, who took it 16 yards to the end zone, giving the Saints their first lead of the game at 13–10.

Manning and the Colts answered with their own touchdown drive, moving the ball 76 yards in ten plays. Clark caught 3 passes for 45 yards, while Joseph Addai finished the drive off with a 4-yard touchdown run to put the Colts back on top 17–13 with 6:05 remaining in the quarter. For the just the second time in Super Bowl history both teams scored touchdowns on their initial possessions of the second half; the only other time occurred in Super Bowl XIV.

Hartley would bring the Saints to within one point of tying the game at 17–16, with his third field goal, launched from 47 yards away. In doing so he became the first kicker in Super Bowl history to score three field goals of 40 or more yards in one game.

This was the first one-point lead after the third quarter in Super Bowl history and second closest game after three quarters, behind Super Bowl XXXIX which was tied between the New England Patriots and Philadelphia Eagles.

Fourth quarter

Indianapolis responded with a drive to the New Orleans 33-yard line, only to have Stover miss a 51-yard field goal attempt, giving the ball back to the Saints with good field position on their 41-yard line. After that, Brees led the Saints on another touchdown drive featuring seven different players getting the ball. Bush started off the drive with a 12-yard run, and then Devery Henderson caught a pass on the Colts' 36-yard line. Following an 8-yard catch and run by Bush, Brees completed passes to Colston, Robert Meachem and tight end David Thomas, moving the ball to the 5-yard line. After a 3-yard run by Pierre Thomas, Brees threw a 2-yard touchdown pass to tight end Jeremy Shockey. Rather than settle for a six point lead, and risk a potential Colts game-winning touchdown, the Saints chanced a two-point conversion. Lance Moore received a pass and attempted to stretch the ball out over the goal line as he fell to the ground and rolled over on his head. The ball was kicked away from his hands by defender Jacob Lacey, and the play was ruled an incomplete pass, prompting a coach's challenge from Sean Payton. After the review, the ruling on the field was overturned when it was determined that Moore maintained possession of the ball long enough and the ball had crossed the plane of the goal line for a successful conversion, giving the Saints a 24–17 advantage.

On the ensuing drive, Manning led the Colts into Saints territory; however, Tracy Porter intercepted a pass by Manning at the Saints 26 for the first takeaway of the game and returned it 74 yards for a touchdown; following the successful extra point, the Saints lead grew to 31–17 with 3:12 remaining. Porter's interception return for a touchdown improved teams to 10–0 in Super Bowls when returning an interception for a touchdown.

Now down by two possessions, the Colts needed a touchdown on their next drive to stay alive, though they still had all three of their timeouts to use. They were able to drive to the New Orleans 3 yard line. When an offensive pass interference penalty on 1st and goal pushed them back 10 yards, the Colts got those 10 yards back on the next play. The next three plays saw a tipped pass that went off of the goal post and incomplete, a loss of two yards on a rushing play, and a pass that went through the hands of wide receiver Reggie Wayne and incomplete, effectively sealing the win for the Saints and giving them their first league championship in franchise history.

Scoring summary

Scoring Play	Score
1st Quarter	
IND – Matt Stover 38 yard field goal, 7:29	IND 3–0
IND – Pierre Garçon 19 yard pass from Peyton Manning (Matt Stover kick), 0:36	IND 10–0
2nd Quarter	
NO – Garrett Hartley 46 yard field goal, 9:34	IND 10–3
NO – Garrett Hartley 44 yard field goal, 0:00	IND 10–6
3rd Quarter	
NO – Pierre Thomas 16 yard pass from Drew Brees (Garrett Hartley kick), 11:41	NO 13–10
IND – Joseph Addai 4 yard run (Matt Stover kick), 6:05	IND 17–13
NO – Garrett Hartley 47 yard field goal, 2:01	IND 17–16
4th Quarter	
NO – Jeremy Shockey 2 yard pass from Drew Brees (Drew Brees pass to Lance Moore), 5:42	NO 24–17
NO – Tracy Porter 74 yard interception return (Garrett Hartley kick), 3:12	NO 31–17

Statistics

Drew Brees was named Super Bowl MVP for tying a Super Bowl record by completing 32 of 39 passes, with 288 passing yards and two touchdowns. After the game, Brees said, "Four years ago, who ever thought this would be happening when 85 percent of the city was under water? Most people left not knowing if New Orleans would ever come back, or if the organization would ever come back. We just all looked at one another and said, 'We are going to rebuild together. We are going to lean on each other.' This is the culmination in all that belief."

Source: NFL.com [1]	New Orleans Saints	Indianapolis Colts
First downs	20	23
Third down efficiency	3/9	6/13
Fourth down efficiency	0/1	1/2
Total yards	332	432
Passing yards	281	333
Passing – completions/attempts	32/39	31/45

Rushing yards	51	99
Rushing attempts	18	19
Yards per rush	2.8	5.2
Penalties–yards	3–19	5–45
Sacks against–yards	1–7	0–0
Fumbles–lost	0–0	0–0
Interceptions thrown	0	1
Time of possession	30:11	29:49

Individual leaders

Saints Passing			
	C/ATT[*]	Yds	TD	INT
Drew Brees	32/39	288	2	0

Saints Rushing			
	Car[a]	Yds	TD	LG[b]
Pierre Thomas	9	30	0	7
Reggie Bush	5	25	0	12
Mike Bell	2	4	0	4
Drew Brees	1	–1	0	–1
Devery Henderson	1	–7	0	–7

Saints Receiving			
	Rec[c]	Yds	TD	LG[b]
Marques Colston	7	83	0	27
Devery Henderson	7	63	0	19
Pierre Thomas	6	55	1	16
Reggie Bush	4	38	0	16
Lance Moore	2	21	0	21
Jeremy Shockey	3	13	1	7
David Thomas	1	9	0	9
Robert Meachem	2	6	0	6

Saints Defense				
	Tak/Ast/Tot[t]	Int	Ff[g]	Sck
Jonathan Vilma	7/0/7	0	0	0.0
Roman Harper	6/1/7	0	0	0.0
Scott Shanle	5/1/6	0	0	0.0
Malcolm Jenkins	4/0/4	0	0	0.0
Tracy Porter	4/0/4	1	0	0.0
Sedrick Ellis	3/0/3	0	0	0.0
Scott Fujita	3/1/4	0	0	0.0
Jabari Greer	3/1/4	0	0	0.0
Randall Gay	2/0/2	0	0	0.0
Anthony Hargrove	2/1/3	0	0	0.0
Bobby McCray	2/0/2	0	0	0.0
Darren Sharper	2/1/1	0	0	0.0
Jeff Charleston	1/0/1	0	0	0.0
Will Smith	1/0/1	0	0	0.0

Colts Passing				
	C/ATT[*]	Yds	TD	INT
Peyton Manning	31/45	333	1	1
Colts Rushing				
	Car[a]	Yds	TD	LG[b]
Joseph Addai	13	77	1	26
Donald Brown	4	18	0	5
Mike Hart	2	4	0	4
Colts Receiving				
	Rec[c]	Yds	TD	LG[b]
Dallas Clark	7	86	0	27
Austin Collie	6	66	0	40
Pierre Garçon	5	66	1	19

Joseph Addai	7		58	0	17
Reggie Wayne	5		46	0	14
Donald Brown	1		11	0	11

Colts Defense				
	Tak/Ast/Tot[t]	Int	Ff[g]	Sck
Gary Brackett	12/1/13	0	0	0.0
Jacob Lacey	6/0/6	0	0	0.0
Melvin Bullitt	5/0/5	0	0	0.0
Kelvin Hayden	5/1/6	0	0	0.0
Antoine Bethea	4/0/4	0	0	0.0
Tim Jennings	3/0/3	0	0	0.0
Clint Session	3/2/5	0	0	0.0
Eric Foster	2/0/2	0	0	0.0
Raheem Brock	1/0/1	0	0	0.0
Dwight Freeney	1/0/1	0	0	1.0
Antonio Johnson	1/1/2	0	0	0.0
Daniel Muir	1/0/1	0	0	0.0
Jerraud Powers	1/1/2	0	0	0.0
Keyunta Dawson	0/1/1	0	0	0.0

[*]Completions/Attempts [a]Carries [b]Long play [c]Receptions [t]Tackles [g]Forced Fumble

- New Orleans recorded the first onside kick attempt in a Super Bowl outside of the fourth quarter.
- Indianapolis' place kicker Matt Stover became the oldest player to participate, as well as to score, in a Super Bowl at 42 years and 11 days of age.
- New Orleans' place kicker Garrett Hartley became the first kicker in Super Bowl history to kick three field goals of 40 or more yards.
- New Orleans' victory marked the sixth straight Super Bowl won by the team wearing its white jersey.
- New Orleans quarterback Drew Brees had the second highest completion percentage in Super Bowl history (Phil Simms in Super Bowl XXI has the highest.) Brees also tied the mark for most completions in a Super Bowl, with 32.
- This was the first Super Bowl played in Sun Life Stadium not to have a kickoff returned for a touchdown.

- New Orleans became the second team to win the Super Bowl after trailing at halftime AND failing to score a first-half touchdown. The New York Giants in Super Bowl XLII are the only other team to do so.
- The Saints' 25 points in the second half is the fourth highest total in Super Bowl history. The New York Giants scored 30 in Super Bowl XXI while 28 was scored by both the San Francisco 49ers in Super Bowl XXIV and the Tampa Bay Buccaneers in Super Bowl XXXVII.
- The Saints also became the seventh team to win a Super Bowl after trailing to start the fourth quarter. The others to do so were: the Giants in Super Bowl XLII, the 49ers in Super Bowl XXIII, the Washington Redskins in Super Bowl XVII, the Pittsburgh Steelers in Super Bowls X and XIV and the Colts in Super Bowl V.
- Brees and Peyton Manning combined for a Super Bowl record 75% completion rate (63 of 84). They also accounted for the most combined pass completions in a Super Bowl, with 63.
- The Colts became just the fifth team to score 10 or more points in the first quarter and lose the game, joining the Miami Dolphins in Super Bowl XIX, the Denver Broncos in both Super Bowls XXI and XXII, and the New England Patriots in Super Bowl XXXI
- Having been down 10 points in the first quarter, the Saints tied a record for the biggest comeback win in Super Bowl history, set in Super Bowl XXII when the Washington Redskins faced a 10-point first quarter deficit of their own.
- The Saints are the 9th team to win the Super Bowl on their first attempt. The others are the Green Bay Packers of Super Bowl I, the Pittsburgh Steelers of Super Bowl IX, the New York Jets of Super Bowl III, the San Francisco 49ers of Super Bowl XVI, the Chicago Bears of Super Bowl XX, the New York Giants of Super Bowl XXI, the Baltimore Ravens of Super Bowl XXXV, and the Tampa Bay Buccaneers of Super Bowl XXXVII.

Starting lineups

New Orleans	Position	Position	Indianapolis
OFFENSE			
Marques Colston	WR		Reggie Wayne
Jermon Bushrod	LT		Charlie Johnson
Carl Nicks	LG		Ryan Lilja
Jonathan Goodwin	C		Jeff Saturday
Jahri Evans	RG		Kyle DeVan
Jon Stinchcomb	RT		Ryan Diem
Jeremy Shockey	TE		Dallas Clark
Devery Henderson	WR		Pierre Garcon

Drew Brees	QB		Peyton Manning
Pierre Thomas	RB		Joseph Addai
Reggie Bush	RB	FB	Gijon Robinson
DEFENSE			
Bobby McCray	LE		Robert Mathis
Sedrick Ellis	DT	LDT	Daniel Muir
Will Smith	RE	RDT	Antonio Johnson
Marvin Mitchell	ILB	RE	Dwight Freeney
Scott Fujita	LOLB		Philip Wheeler
Jonathan Vilma	ILB		Gary Brackett
Scott Shanle	ROLB		Clint Session
Jabari Greer	LCB		Kelvin Hayden
Tracy Porter	RCB		Jacob Lacey
Roman Harper	SS		Melvin Bullitt
Darren Sharper	FS		Antoine Bethea

Officials

- Referee – Scott Green (#19)
- Umpire – Undrey Wash (#96)
- Head Linesman – John McGrath (#5)
- Line Judge – Jeff Seeman (#45)
- Field Judge – Rob Vernatchi (#75)
- Side Judge – Greg Meyer (#78)
- Back Judge – Greg Steed (#12)
- Alt. referee – Gene Steratore (#114)

Game time and weather conditions

- Kickoff was at 6:32 p.m. EST (23:32 UTC).
- Weather at kickoff was , clear.
- Game length was 3 hrs. 14 min.

External links

- NFL.com's official Super Bowl website [2]
- Host committee website [3]
- Super Bowl XLIV at ESPN [4]

Drew Brees

Drew Brees

Andrew Christopher "Drew" Brees (; born January 15, 1979) is the starting quarterback for the New Orleans Saints of the National Football League. He was drafted by the San Diego Chargers in the second round of the 2001 NFL Draft. He played college football at Purdue.

Brees has been selected to the Pro Bowl four times in his career – with the Chargers in 2004 and the Saints in 2006, 2008, and 2009. He was named the NFL's Comeback Player of the Year in 2004, the Offensive Player of the Year in 2008, and the MVP of Super Bowl XLIV. He was also selected by voters to appear on the cover of Electronic Arts' *Madden NFL 11*.

High school

He went 28-0-1 in his two years as a starting quarterback at Westlake High School in Austin, Texas. He won the state championship with Westlake High School and also holds many records there.

College career

Brees graduated from Purdue University with a degree in Industrial Management. He left Purdue with Big Ten Conference records in passing yards (11,792), touchdown passes (90), total offensive yards (12,693), completions (1,026), and attempts (1,678). He led the Boilermakers to the 2001 Rose Bowl, Purdue's first appearance there since 1967. In the game Purdue lost by ten points to the Washington Huskies. Brees was a finalist for the Davey O'Brien Award as the nation's best quarterback in 1999. He won the Maxwell Award as the nation's outstanding player of 2000 and won the NCAA's Today's Top VIII Award as a member of the Class of 2001. Brees was also fourth in Heisman Trophy voting in 1999 and third in 2000.

As a senior, Brees was named the Academic All-America Player of Year, the first Purdue player since Bruce Brineman (1989) to earn national academic honors. Brees also was awarded Purdue's Leonard Wilson Award for unselfishness and dedication.

Professional career

San Diego Chargers

2001 NFL Draft

Brees' college success led to projections that he would be a mid-to-late first round draft pick in the 2001 NFL Draft, but he slipped due to concerns about his relatively short stature for a professional quarterback (6'0"), a perceived lack of arm strength, and a sense that he had succeeded in college in a system designed for him. Ultimately, Brees was the second quarterback selected in the 2001 draft, chosen by the San Diego Chargers as the first pick of the second round.

San Diego originally had the first pick in that draft, but traded it to Atlanta (which used it to draft Michael Vick) in return for the fifth pick of the first round, with which San Diego drafted LaDainian Tomlinson.

Early career

Brees played in his first professional game on November 4, 2001 against the Kansas City Chiefs. He had won the starting job over Doug Flutie during training camp before the start of the 2002 season, but was later replaced during the 2003 season by Flutie.

Brees' career with the Chargers was put in jeopardy after San Diego acquired NC State's Philip Rivers. After the trade, it was almost certain Brees' days as the Chargers' starting QB were over. However, Rivers held out nearly all of training camp. This forced the Chargers coaching staff to give Brees one last look and he remained the starter throughout the 2004 season. Brees was selected to the 2005 NFL Pro Bowl following an impressive 2004 season in which the Chargers won the AFC West. He was named 2004 NFL Comeback Player of the Year.

2005

Brees became a free agent after the season and was not expected to return to San Diego, which had already committed a large sum of money to Rivers. The team eventually designated Brees a franchise player, giving him a one-year contract that quadrupled his pay to $8 million for 2005.

Under the terms of the franchise player contract, Brees was eligible to be traded or sign with another team, but the Chargers would have had to receive two future first round draft choices in return. He was not traded and continued to start the remainder of the 2005 season.

Brees continued his productive play in 2005, as he posted a career high in passing yards with 3,576. Brees also posted an 89.2 rating, 10th best in the NFL. However, in the last game of the 2005 season against the Denver Broncos, Brees injured his shoulder while trying to pick up his own fumble after being hit by Broncos safety John Lynch. Denver tackle Gerard Warren hit Brees while he was on the ground, causing the injury. Brees underwent arthroscopic surgery to repair the torn labrum in his right (throwing) shoulder on January 5, 2006. Subsequent reports mention additional rotator cuff damage.

Brees was selected as first alternate to the AFC Pro Bowl team for the 2005 season. He would have played in his second consecutive Pro Bowl due to the injury to starter Carson Palmer, but his own injury dictated that the AFC Pro Bowl roster would have to be filled by second alternate Jake Plummer.

After the season, the Chargers offered Brees a 5-year, $50 million contract that paid $2 million in base salary the first year and the rest heavily based on performance incentives. Brees took the incentive-based offer as a sign of no confidence by the Chargers and promptly demanded the type of money a top 5 "franchise" quarterback would receive.

New Orleans Saints

After the Chargers refused to increase their offer, Brees met with other teams. The New Orleans Saints and the Miami Dolphins were interested. New Orleans made an offer that included $10 million in guaranteed money the first year and a $12 million option the second year. Miami was unsure if Brees' shoulder was completely healed and did not offer the money Brees was seeking. The Dolphins ended negotiations and traded for Minnesota Vikings QB Daunte Culpepper instead. Brees signed a 6-year, $60 million deal with the Saints on March 14, 2006.

2006

Brees had a productive first year with the Saints, as the team, under first-year head coach Sean Payton, rebounded from its disastrous 2005 season (when the team was unable to play in New Orleans due to the damage caused by Hurricane Katrina and struggled to a 3-13 record) to finish with a 10-6 regular season record and won the NFC South division title. Brees threw a league-leading 4,418 passing yards, finished third in the league with 26 touchdown passes and 11 interceptions and a 96.2 passer rating. Brees was named starting quarterback for the NFC in the 2007 Pro Bowl. On January 5, 2007, Brees was named first runner-up behind former teammate Tomlinson for league MVP by the Associated Press. Brees and Tomlinson were co-recipients of the Walter Payton Man of the Year Award.

On January 13, 2007, in his first playoff game for New Orleans, Brees was 20-32 in passing attempts with 1 touchdown and no interceptions against the Philadelphia Eagles in the Louisiana Superdome. The Saints held on to win 27-24, and advanced to the franchise's first NFC Championship Game against the Chicago Bears. Though he completed 27 of 49 passes for 354 yards against the Chicago Bears, and two touchdowns, Brees committed three costly turnovers, and was penalized for an intentional grounding in the endzone, resulting in a safety, as the Saints lost 39-14. Brees then dislocated his left elbow during the first quarter of the Pro Bowl.

2007

The following season Brees passed for 4428 yards and tied a then team record with 28 touchdowns. He also set the NFL record previously held by Rich Gannon for pass completions in a single season with 440. However, the Saints missed the playoffs.

2008

In 2008, the Saints again missed the playoffs but Brees had a strong year statistically, finishing 15 yards short of the NFL record for passing yards thrown in a single season set by Dan Marino in 1984. He finished the season with 5,069 yards and became the second quarterback in NFL history to throw for over 5,000 yards in a season. He passed for 300 yards ten times during the season, tying Rich Gannon's 2002 record. He was named FedEx Air Player of the Week for his performances during weeks 8 and 12 and was named the AP 2008 Offensive Player of the Year.

2009 Super Bowl Season

In the first game of the 2009 season against the Detroit Lions, Brees set a career-high and franchise-tying record with six touchdown passes, going 26/34 for 358 yards. He also set a league record for most passing touchdowns on opening weekend. The next week, Brees led the Saints to a 48-22 win over the Philadelphia Eagles, throwing for 311 yards and three touchdown passes. Brees also tied the record for most touchdown passes by the end of week 2 with 9. In week 6 against the 5-0 New York Giants, Brees completed 23 of 30 passes for 369 yards, 4 touchdown passes and a passer rating of 156.8 in a dominant 48-27 victory.

In week 7, Brees led a dramatic comeback victory on the road against the Miami Dolphins, 46-34. The Saints quickly faced a 24-3 deficit in the second quarter, trailing for the first time all season at that point, and failing to score on their first possession as they had in all of their previous contests. Brees had a poor outing, but provided two crucial rushing touchdowns, one just before the second half to narrow the deficit to 24-10, and one in the third quarter to give the Saints their first lead of the game, 37-34.

The next week, Brees threw for 308 yards on 25 of 33 passing along with two touchdowns and one interception in leading the Saints to a 35-27 victory and franchise tying best start at 7-0 against the rival Atlanta Falcons. In week 9, Brees helped guide the team to a 30-20 victory over the Carolina Panthers. This would be Drew's first victory over the Carolina Panthers in the Superdome and allowed the Saints to take their best ever start in franchise history at 8-0.

In week 12, Brees led the Saints to an 11-0 record, defeating the New England Patriots 38-17 on *Monday Night Football*. Drew Brees totaled 371 yards passing, posting a perfect passer rating of 158.3.

After close victories over the Washington Redskins and Falcons in successive weeks to start 13-0, Brees and the Saints lost their first game of the season to the Dallas Cowboys, 24-17, after DeMarcus Ware caused a Brees fumble in the final seconds, ending a fourth quarter rally. The Saints would then lose their last two games, with Brees sitting out the week 17 finale against Carolina. Their 13-3 record secured the #1 seed in the NFC.

Brees' individual statistics led to numerous accolades, including a Pro Bowl selection, the Maxwell Football Club's Bert Bell Award, and runner-up in voting for the AP MVP, Offensive Player of the Year, and All-Pro awards. He finished the season with a completion percentage of 70.62, establishing a new NFL record.

In the divisional round of the playoffs, the Saints routed the Arizona Cardinals 45-14 to advance to the NFC Championship, where they defeated the Minnesota Vikings 31-28 in overtime. Brees completed 17 of 31 passes for 191 yards and 3 touchdowns.

The underdog Saints defeated the Indianapolis Colts 31-17 in Super Bowl XLIV on February 7, 2010. Brees tied a Super Bowl record with 32 pass completions and won the Super Bowl Most Valuable Player Award. He threw for 288 yards and 2 touchdowns. It was the first league championship in Saints franchise history.

Career statistics

Year	Team	G-S	Passing Att.-Comp.	Yards	Pct.	TD	Int.	Long	Sacks-Lost	Pass Rating
2001	San Diego	1-0	27-15	221	.556	1	0	40	2-12	94.8
2002	San Diego	16-16	526-320	3,284	.608	17	16	52	24-180	76.9
2003	San Diego	11-11	356-205	2,108	.576	11	15	68	21-178	67.5
2004	San Diego	15-15	400-262	3,159	.655	27	7	79	18-131	104.8
2005	San Diego	16-16	500-323	3,576	.646	24	15	54	27-223	89.2
2006	New Orleans	16-16	554-356	4,418	.643	26	11	86	18-105	96.2
2007	New Orleans	16-16	652-440	4,423	.675	28	18	58	16-109	89.4
2008	New Orleans	16-16	635-413	5,069	.650	34	17	84	13-92	96.2
2009	New Orleans	15-15	514-363	4,388	.706	34	11	75	20-135	109.6
Totals		122-121	4,164-2,697	30,646	.648	202	110	86	159-1,165	91.9
Postseason		6-6	225-150	1648	.667	13	2	88	10-61	103.7

San Diego Chargers franchise records

- Highest Comp. %, Season (Min. 14 attempts/game) - 65.5% (2004)
- Highest Comp. %, Game (Min. 20 attempts) - 88.0% vs. Oakland 10/31/2004
- Highest Comp. %, Playoff Game (Min. 10 attempts) - 73.8% vs. NY Jets 1/8/2005
- Most Consecutive Attempts, None Intercepted - 194 (Oct. 17 through Dec. 5 2004)

New Orleans Saints franchise records

- Highest Comp. %, Career (Min. 500 attempts) - 65.7%
- Highest Comp. %, Season (Min. 14 attempts/game) - 70.62% (2009)
- Highest YPA, Career (Min. 500 attempts) - 7.56
- Highest YPA, Season (Min. 14 attempts/game) - 8.5 (2009)
- Highest Passer Rating, Career (Min. 500 attempts) - 93.8
- Highest Passer Rating, Season (Min. 14 attempts/game) - 109.6 (2009)
- Most Completions, Season - 440 (2007)
- Most Completions, Game - 39 vs. Denver, 9/21/2008
- Most Consecutive Completions - 19 (12/27/09)
- Most Pass Attempts, Season - 652 (2007)
- Most Pass Attempts, Game - 60 (tied with Aaron Brooks)
- Most Passing Yards, Season - 5069 (2008) (Second in NFL history)
- Most Passing Yards, Game - 510 vs. Cincinnati, 11/19/2006 (Fifth in NFL history)
- Most 4000 Yard Passing Seasons - 4
- Most Consecutive 4000 Yard Passing Seasons - 4 (2006-09)
- Most Games w/300+ Yards Passing, Season - 10 (2008)
- Most Consecutive Games w/300+ Yards Passing - 5 (2006)
- Most Touchdown Passes, Season - 34 (2008 and 2009)
- Most Touchdown Passes, Game - 6 (9/13/2009) (tied with Billy Kilmer)
- Most Touchdown Passes On Opening Day, 6 (2009)
- Most Touchdown Passes, Career - 122

National Football League records

- Most completions, season - 440 (2007)
- Highest completion percentage, season - 70.62% (2009)
- Highest completion percentage, career postseason - 66.67% (150/225)
- Lowest interception percentage, career postseason - 0.89%
- Most completions in a Super Bowl (tied with Tom Brady) - 32 (Super Bowl XLIV)

Personal life

Brees was born in Dallas, Texas. He and his wife Brittany purchased and renovated a home in Uptown New Orleans.

Brees married his college sweetheart, Brittany Brees, in February 2003. They both met and dated while attending Purdue University.

Brees is allergic to dairy, wheat, gluten, and eggs.

Brees was born with a mole on his right cheek. When Brees was 3, his parents considered having the birthmark removed, but doctors said that there was no medical reason to remove it.

Brees' mother, Mina Brees, died on August 7, 2009 at age 59. The death was ruled a suicide. Brees was briefly excused from training camp for a "family matter." In 2006, Brees described their relationship as "nonexistent" ever since he refused to hire her as his agent when he entered the NFL. After her death, Brees stated that this quote was three years old and that his relationship with his mother had been improving.

Brees and his wife Brittany welcomed their first child, a son named Baylen Robert Brees on January 15, 2009 which was also Brees' 30th birthday.

Brees became a brother of the Sigma Chi Fraternity while at Purdue.

Brees could have gone to Brown University, and said that if he had, he might be in politics right now. His host on a recruiting visit was Sean Morey, a former Pro Bowler for Arizona Cardinals.

In April 2010, Brees was voted by fans as the cover athlete of EA Sports upcoming Madden NFL 11 video game.

On April 23, 2010 in an interview with Live with Regis and Kelly, Brees confirmed that his wife was pregnant with the couple's second child, which is another boy. The baby is due in October 2010.

On July 6, 2010, in an interview with Good Morning America, Brees again confirmed that he and his wife are expecting another child together, and he discussed his new book, released that same day. The book, entitled *Coming Back Stronger: Unleashing the Hidden Power of Adversity*, is co-authored by Chris Fabry and published by Tyndale House. *Coming Back Stronger* opened at number 3 on the non-fiction bestseller list of *The New York Times*.

Charity and volunteer activities

As a result of both his on-field success with the Saints and his extensive charitable activities since arriving in New Orleans, Brees has become (in the words of a 2010 *Sports Illustrated* profile) "an athlete as adored and appreciated as any in an American city today". He has been involved in Hurricane Katrina recovery. Drew and Brittany's Brees Dream Foundation [1] announced a partnership in 2007 with international children's charity Operation Kids, to rebuild and restore and recreate academic and athletic facilities, parks and playgrounds, after-school programs, mentoring programs for the intellectually disabled, neighborhood revitalization projects and child care facilities in New Orleans.

Brees has acquired the nickname "Breesus" among Saints fans.

Brees visited the Guantanamo Bay detention camp on a USO tour in late June 2009. Following his return, Brees was quoted as stating that Guantanamo captives were being treated ten times better than convicts in U.S. prisons.

In February 2008, Brees signed a promotional deal with Chili's Grill & Bar to promote the chain's new line of hamburgers. The promotion helped raise money for charity. In June 2008, Brees participated in the Pro Sports Team Challenge, a competition for pro athletes to help raise money for charities. The charity Brees played for was Operation Kids.

On February 18, 2007, Brees was honored by the Krewe of Bacchus, a New Orleans Mardi Gras parade club,as the 2007 Bacchus Grand Marshal.

Brees again presided as Bacchus during the 2010 parade on February 14, 2010, one week after the Super Bowl during Mardi Gras season.

In June 2010, President Obama appointed Brees to be co-chair of the newly renamed President's Council on Fitness, Sports, and Nutrition, along with former Olympic gymnast Dominique Dawes.

In 2010, as a result of the Deepwater Horizon oil spill, Brees appeared in a commercial to raise awareness for the spill. Also starring in the commercial were Sandra Bullock, Peyton and Eli Manning, Jack Del Rio, Emeril Lagasse, James Carville, Blake Lively, and John Goodman.

See also

- NFL career passer rating leaders
- List of NFL Quarterbacks who have passed for 400 or more yards
- List of NFL quarterbacks who have posted a perfect passer rating
- List of 300-Yard Passing Games by NFL Quarterbacks
- Most wins by a starting quarterback (NFL)
- NFL QB Playoff records as starters

External links

- The Brees Dream Foundation [2]
- New Orleans Saints bio [3]
- ESPN Profile [4]

Players and Head Coaches

List of New Orleans Saints players

This is a **list of American football players who have played for the New Orleans Saints** in the National Football League (NFL). It includes players that have played at least one match in the NFL regular season. The New Orleans Saints franchise was originally founded in 1967. The Saints made their first franchise Super Bowl appearance in 2010, have one conference championship, and have three division championships.

A

Sarah Abadie, Danny Abramowicz, Dick Absher, Tom Ackerman, Michael Adams, Sam Adams, Scott Adams, Vashone Adams, Margene Adkins, Ink Aleaga, Vincent Alexander, Eric Allen, James Allen, Kenderick Allen, Terry Allen, Gerald Alphin, Ashley Ambrose, Morten Andersen, Dick Anderson, Gary Anderson, Jesse Anderson, Sheldon Andrus, Tyrone Anthony, Bert Askson, Pete Athas, Doug Atkins, Gene Atkins, Cliff Austin

B

Tom Backes, Melvin Baker, Tony Baker, Gordon Banks, Derrick Barnes, Tommy Barnhardt, Malcolm Barnwell, Tom Barrington, Don Bass, Mario Bates, Steve Baumgartner, John Beasley, Brett Bech, Carlos Bell, Jay Bellamy, Wes Bender, Guy Benjamin, Barry Bennett, Monte Bennett, Cliff Benson, LeCharles Bentley, Mitch Berger, Dwight Beverly, Jeff Blake, Cary Blanchard, Tom Blanchard, Dwaine Board, Colby Bockwoldt, Jim Boeke, Chris Bordano, Ken Bordelon, Wade Bosarge, Kirk Botkin, Todd Bouman, Jerry Boyarsky, Greg Boyd, Greg Boykin, McKinley Boykin, Jamaal Branch, Robert Brannon, Drew Brees, Hoby Brenner, Johnny Brewer, Doug Brien, Stan Brock, Aaron Brooks, Willie Broughton, Bob Brown, Charlie Brown, Derek Brown, Fakhir Brown, Jammal Brown, Ray Brown, Mark Brunell Tony Bryant, Mike Buck, Vince Buck, Josh Bullocks, Don Burchfield, Vern Burke, Jackie Burkett, Ed Burns, Bo Burris, Ken Burrough, Larry Burton, Reggie Bush, Jermon Bushrod, Bill Butler, Skip Butler, Israel Byrd

C

Earl Campbell, Joe Campbell, Mark Campbell, James Campen, Chris Canty, Warren Capone, John Carney, Tom Carr, Herman Carroll, Travis Carroll, Wesley Carroll, Dale Carter, David Carter, Ki-Jana Carter, Tim Carter, Craig Cassady, Rich Caster, Rusty Chambers, Wes Chandler, Clarence Chapman, Gil Chapman, Jeff Charleston, Martin Chase, Jesse Chatman, Je'Rod Cherry, Henry Childs, Ron Childs, Larry Cipa, Kendrick Clancy, Bruce Clark, Danny Clark, Kelvin Clark, Robert Clark, Vinnie Clark, Phil Clarke, Willie Clay, Cam Cleeland, Charlie Clemons, Bill Cody, Mike Cofer, Dan Colchico, Don Coleman, Kerry Collins, Larry Collins, Wayne Colman, Marques Colston, Chuck Commiskey, Albert Connell, Darion Conner, Bill Contz, Ernie Conwell, Toi Cook, Larry Coombs, Josh Cooper, Richard Cooper, Terrance Copper, Lou Cordileone, Olie Cordill, Bruce Cortez, Chad Cota, John Covington, Bryan Cox, Curome Cox, Mike Crangle, Jason Craft, Aaron Craver, Keyuo Craver, Bob Creech, Chuck Crist, Sylvester Croom, Ron Crosby, Billy Cundiff, Carl Cunningham, Gary Cuozzo

D

Oakley Dalton, Jason David, Jeff Davidson, Bob Davis, Dave Davis, Dick Davis, Don Davis, Isaac Davis, Norman Davis, Ted Davis, Travis Davis, Travis Davis, Troy Davis, Sean Dawkins, Lawrence Dawsey, Stacey Dawsey, Joe DeForest, Jack DeGrenier, Jack Del Rio, Jake Delhomme, Curtis Deloatch, Tom Dempsey, Lee DeRamus, Jim DeRatt, Glenn Derby, John Didion, Ernest Dixon, Ronnie Dixon, Conrad Dobler, Al Dodd, Jim Dombrowski, Tom Donovan, Andy Dorris, John Douglas, Marques Douglas, Bobby Douglass, Marcus Dowdell, Tyronne Drakeford, Kenny Duckett, Jonathan Dumbauld, Jubilee Dunbar, Karl Dunbar, Vaughn Dunbar, Charlie Durkee, Bill Dusenberry, Duane Dorsey

E

Quinn Early, Brad Edelman, Kelvin Edwards, Ted Elliott, Tony Elliott, Frank Emanuel, Tory Epps, Russell Erxleben, Lawrence Estes, Chuck Evans, Jahri Evans, Troy Evans, Willie Evans, Jim Everett

F

Julian Fagan, Jeff Faine, Chris Farasopoulos, Hap Farber, John Farquhar, Jeff Faulkner, Joe Federspiel, Happy Feller, Eric Felton, James Fenderson, Gill Fenerty, Jim Ferguson, Paul Fersen, Ross Fichtner, Jitter Fields, Mark Fields, Bill Fifer, Alfred Fincher, Mike Fink, Roger Finnie, Levar Fisher, Jim Flanigan, Spencer Folau, Jerry Fontenot, Henry Ford, James Ford, Brian Forde, John Fourcade, Keith Fourcade, Bobby Fowler, P. J. Franklin, Todd Franz, Jim Fraser, Paul Frazier, Reggie Freeman, Toni Fritsch, Johnny Fuller, Mike Fultz

G

Hokie Gajan, Tony Galbreath, Kendall Gammon, Wayne Gandy, Jim Garcia, Talman Gardner, Len Garrett, Russell Gary, James Geathers, Ronnie Ghent, Donnie Gibbs, Antonio Gibson, Daren Gilbert, John Gilliam, Steve Gleason, Vencie Glenn, Andrew Glover, La'Roi Glover, Robert Goff, Dan Goich, Eugene Goodlow, Jonathan Goodwin, Darren Gottschalk, Toby Gowin, Hoyle Granger, Charles Grant, Cie Grant, Cecil Gray, David Gray, Kevin Gray, Leon Gray, Mel Gray, Arthur Green, Howard Green, Paul Green, Victor Green, Donovan Greer, Ted Gregory, Bob Gresham, DeJuan Groce, Elois Grooms, Earl Gros, Lee Gross, Jeff Groth, Terry Guess, Eric Guliford, Mark Gunn, Ross Gwinn

H

Az-Zahir Hakim, Mike Halapin, Lamont Hall, Tom Hall, Willie Hall, Andy Hamilton, Uhuru Hamiter, Norman Hand, Jim Hanna, Brian Hansen, Greg Harding, Larry Hardy, Edd Hargett, Deveron Harper, Roman Harper, Bill Harris, Corey Harris, Herbert Harris, Ike Harris, Rod Harris, Victor Harrison, Ben Hart, Jeff Hart, Tommy Hart, Garrett Hartley, George Harvey, Richard Harvey, Jr. Richard Harvey, Sr. Andre Hastings, Kevin Haverdink, Sam Havrilak, Michael Hawthorne, Billie Hayes, Mercury Hayes, James Haynes, Michael Haynes (DT), Michael Haynes (WR), Major Hazelton, Bobby Hebert, Devery Henderson, Jimmy Heidel, Othello Henderson, Don Herrmann, Jim Hester, Ray Hester, Chris Hewitt, Craig Heyward, Jay Hilgenberg, Joel Hilgenberg, John Hill, Lonzell Hill, Randal Hill, Dalton Hilliard, Keno Hills, Zachary Hilton, Glen Ray Hines, Terry Hoage, Billy Hobbs, Daryl Hobbs, Billy Joe Hobert, Milford Hodge, Sedrick Hodge, Tommy Hodson, Augie Hoffmann, Curtis Holden, Sam Holden, Montrae Holland, Hugo Hollas, Stan Holloway, Jack Holmes, Chris Horn, Joe Horn, Aaron Hosack, Derrick Hoskins, Kevin Houser, Walter Housman, Darren Howard, Gene Howard, Reggie Howard, Delles Howell, John Huard, Dave Hubbard, Nat Hudson, Pat Hughes, Tyrone Hughes, Kevin Hunt, Earnest Hunter, Bill Hurley, Fred Hyatt

I

Clint Ingram, Kevin Ingram, Ken Irvin, Qadry Ismail, Steve Israel

J

Ernie Jackson, Grady Jackson, Greg Jackson, Jonathan Jackson, Rickey Jackson, Willie Jackson, Harry Jacobs, Kendyl Jacox, Van Jakes, Philip James, Garland Jean-Batiste, Haywood Jeffires, Dameian Jeffries, Stanford Jennings, Paul Jetton, Alonzo Johnson, Benny Johnson, Bobby Johnson Carl Johnson, Dirk Johnson, Earl Johnson, Eric Johnson, J. R. Johnson, Joe Johnson, John Johnson, Nate Johnson, Tony Johnson, Tyrone Johnson, Undra Johnson, Vaughan Johnson, Walter Johnson, Andrew Jones, Brian Jones, Clarence Jones, Donta Jones, Ernest Jones, J. J. Jones, Jamal Jones, Jerry Jones, Kim Jones, Mike Jones, Ray Jones, Reginald Jones, Selwyn Jones, Tebucky Jones, Buford Jordan,

Jimmy Jordan, Keith Joseph, Tom Jurich

K

Kevin Kaesviharn, Ken Kaplan, Mike Karney, Jim Kearney, Curtis Keaton, Mike Keim, Les Kelley, Mike Kelly, Rob Kelly, Florian Kempf, Derek Kennard, Eddie Kennison, Billy Kilmer, Elbert Kimbrough, Ed King, Rick Kingrea, Alan Kline, Greg Knafelc, Roger Knight, Sammy Knight, Shawn Knight, David Knowles, Joe Kohlbrand, David Kopay, Steve Korte, Jim Kovach, Kent Kramer, Tommy Kramer, John Krimm, Jake Kupp, Jake Kuresa, Bob Kuziel

L

Dave Lafary, Morris LaGrand, Antwan Lake, Phil LaPorta, Babe Laufenberg, Nate Lawrie, Odell Lawson, Josh "Bernard" Lay, Bill Leach, Scott Leach, Bivian Lee, Carl Lee, Mark Lee, Tyrone Legette, Brad Leggett, Earl Leggett, Lance Legree, Rodney Leisle, Mike Lemon, Derrick Lewis, Gary Lewis (DL), Gary Lewis (RB), Marvin Lewis, Michael Lewis, Reggie Lewis, Rodney Lewis, John Leypoldt, Errol Linden, Dale Lindsey, Toni Linhart, Louis Lipps, Earl Little, Andy Livingston, Greg Loberg, Obert Logan, Chip Lohmiller, Dave Long, Joe Don Looney, Tony Lorick, Sean Lumpkin, Hendrick Lusk, Chase Lyman, Dicky Lyons

M

Cedric Mack, Milton Mack, Archie Manning, Ken Marchiol, Doug Marrone, Jim Marsalis, Olindo Mare, James Marshall, Chris Martin, D'Artagnan Martin, Eric Martin, Jamie Martin, Wayne Martin, Rich Martini, Robert Massey, Kevin Mathis, Reggie Mathis, Pascal Matla, Henry Matthews, Andy Maurer, Rich Mauti, Brett Maxie, Alvin Maxson, Jermane Mayberry, Michael Mayes, Rueben Mayes, Fred McAfee, Deuce McAllister, Don McCall, Bill McClard, J. J. McCleskey, Andy McCollum, Dave McCormick, Larry McCoy, Fred McCrary, Earl McCullouch, Wayne McGarity, Phil McGeoghan, Ralph McGill, Gene McGuire, Toddrick McIntosh, Corey McIntyre, Mike McKenzie, Ronald McKinnon, Dana McLemore, Mark McMillian, Rod McNeill, Tom McNeill, Adrian McPherson, Leon McQuay, Robert Meachem, Terrence Melton, Guido Merkens, Jim Merlo, Casey Merrill, Mark Meseroll, Darren Mickell, Rick Middleton, Steve Mike-Mayer, Billy Miller, Junior Miller, Les Miller, Mike Miller, Sam Mills, Brian Milne, Lincoln Minor, Derrell Mitchell, Keith Mitchell, Kevin Mitchell, Marvin Mitchell, Mel Mitchell, Alex Molden, Derrius Monroe, Marv Montgomery, Monte Montgomery, Doug Mooers, Derland Moore, Eric Moore, Jerald Moore, Jerry Moore, Lance Moore, Reynaud Moore, John Mooring, Mike Morgan, Chris Morris, Don Morrison, Bobby Morse, Thomas Morstead, Chad Morton, Chuck Muncie, Brad Muster, Tommy Myers, DeShone Myles

N

Chris Naeole, Rob Nairne, Lorenzo Neal, Richard Neal, Derrick Ned, Jamar Nesbit, Elijah Nevett, Robert Newkirk, Bob Newland, Anthony Newman, Patrick Newman, Billy Newsome, Richard Newsome, Calvin Nicholson, Rob Ninkovich, Jim Ninowski, Moran Norris, Craig Novitsky, Doug Nussmeier, Vic Nyvall

O

Ken O'Neal, Steve O'Neal, J. T. O'Sullivan, Ray Ogden, Onome Ojo, Chris Oldham, Jim Otis, Louis Oubre, Artie Owens, Joe Owens, John Owens, Tinker Owens

P

Shane Pahukoa, Tyler Palko, Dick Palmer, Emile Palmer, Joel Parker, Steve Parker, Dave Parks, Rick Partridge, Jerome Pathon, Mark Pattison, Whitney Paul, Scott Pelluer, Petey Perot, Brett Perriman, Darren Perry, Vernon Perry, Wilmont Perry, Rob Petitti, Stan Petry, Anwar Phillips, Jess Phillips, Kim Phillips, Dino Philyaw, Jim Pietrzak, Julian Pittman, Elijah Pitts, Ray Poage, Johnnie Poe, Bob Pollard, Tommy Polley, Keith Poole, Nate Poole, Chris Port, Rufus Porter, Marvin Powell, Steve Preece, Elex Price, Marcus Price, Joe Profit, Remi Prudhomme

R

David Rackley, Nate Ramsey, Steve Ramsey, Walter Rasby, Rocky Rasley, Ricky Ray, Ken Reaves, Rusty Rebowe, Glen Redd, Jake Reed, Don Reese, Chris Reis, Mike Rengel, Tutan Reyes, Steve Rhem, Benny Ricardo, Floyd Rice, Mike Richey, Preston Riley, Victor Riley, Tim Riordan, Ray Rissmiller, Marcellus Rivers, Carl Roaches, Willie Roaf, Austin Robbins, Walter Roberts, Craig Robinson, Darien Robinson, Jeff Rodenberger, Derrick Rodgers, Bill Roe, George Rogers, Jimmy Rogers, Steve Rogers, Baron Rollins, George Rose, Scott Ross, Tom Roth, Jim Rourke, Tom Roussel, Dave Rowe, Mark Royals, Orlando Ruff, Paul Ryczek

S

Pio Sagapolutele, Pat Saindon, Bill Sandeman, Scott Sanderson, Bill Saul, Josh Savage, Nicky Savoie, Greg Scales, Joe Scarpati, Roy Schmidt, Terry Schmidt, Adam Schreiber, Randy Schultz, Kurt Schumacher, Don Schwartz, Brian Schweda, Steve Scifres, Bobby Scott, Lindsay Scott, Malcolm Scott, Paul Seal, Kyle Sepulveda, Chad Setterstrom, Siddeeq Shabazz, Scott Shanle, Bob Shaw, Rickie Shaw, Derrick Shepard, John Shinners,Jeremy Shockey Heath Shuler, Don Shy, Ricky Siglar, Brian Simmons, Dave Simmons, Jerry Simmons, Michael Simmons, Mark Simoneau, Ed Simonini, Chuck Slaughter, T. J. Slaughter, David Sloan, Scott Slutzker, Torrance Small, Joel Smeenge, Antowain

Smith, Brady Smith, Cedric Smith, Darrin Smith, Dwight Smith, Irv Smith, Kenny Smith, Lamar Smith, Royce Smith, Shaun Smith, Terrelle Smith, Vinson Smith, Will Smith, Ronnie Lee South, Ernest Spears, Jimmy Spencer, Maurice Spencer, Mike Spivey, Ken Stabler, Dave Stachelski, Donté Stallworth, Israel Stanley, Scott Stauch, Aaron Stecker, Greg Stemrick, Howard Stevens, Jimmy Stewart, Monty Stickles, Terry Stieve, Jon Stinchcomb, Tom Stincic, Fred Stokes, Mike Stonebreaker, Steve Stonebreaker, Omar Stoutmire, Tommie Stowers, Mike Strachan, Eli Strand, Zach Strief, Jim Strong, William Strong, Jerry Sturm, Fred Sturt, Johnathan Sullivan, Doug Sutherland, Jon Sutton, Reggie Sutton, Karl Sweetan, Pat Swilling, Clovis Swinney, Pat Swoopes, Rich Szaro, Dave Szymakowski

T

Don Talbert, Derrick Taylor, James Taylor, Jim Taylor, Keith Taylor, Mike Taylor, Daryl Terrell, Corey Terry, James Thaxton, Charlie Thomas, Curtland Thomas, Fred Thomas, Henry Thomas, Hollis Thomas, Joe Thomas, Joey Thomas, Pierre Thomas, Speedy Thomas, Aundra Thompson, Bennie Thompson, Bobby Thompson, Dave Thompson, Don Thorp, Junior Thurman, John Tice, Mike Tilleman, Faddie Tillman, Richard Todd, Alvin Toles, Billy Joe Tolliver, Jared Tomich, Darrell Toussaint, Willie Townes, Steve Trapilo, Winfred Tubbs, Joe Tuipala, Willie Tullis, Kyle Turley, Renaldo Turnbull, Floyd Turner, Gunnard Twyner, Toussaint Tyler

U

Jeff Uhlenhake

V

Jim Van Wagner, Skip Vanderbundt, Phil Vandersea, Mike Verstegen, Jonathan Vilma

W

Terrence Wagner, Frank Wainright, Dwight Walker, Jeff Walker, Mike Walker, Wesley Walls, Steve Walsh, Carl Ward, Chris Ward, Phillip Ward, Ron Warner, Frank Warren, Dave Washington, Mickey Washington, Mike Waters, Courtney Watson, John Watson, Mike Watson, Frank Wattelet, Dave Waymer, Fred Weary, Steve Weatherford, Cephus Weatherspoon, Ron Weissenhofer, Claxton Welch, Joe Wendryhoski, Greg Westbrooks, Austin Wheatley, Ernie Wheelwright, Creston Whitaker, Mitch White, Willie Whitehead, Dave Whitsell, Fred Whittingham, Ricky Whittle, Tom Wickert, Bob Wicks, Josh Wilcox, Jim Wilks, Boo Williams, Brian Williams, Brooks Williams, Del Williams, James Williams, Joe Williams, John Williams, Larry Williams, Melvin Williams, Ralph Williams, Richard Williams, Ricky Williams, Wally Williams, Willie Williams, Donald Willis, Len Willis, Klaus Wilmsmeyer, Dave Wilson, Jerry Wilson, Ray Wilson, Robert Wilson, Tim Wilson, Troy Wilson,

Wade Wilson, Wayne Wilson, Jeff Winans, Doug Winslow, George Winslow, DeMond Winston, Dennis Winston, Wimpy Winther, Scott Woerner, Gary Wood, John Wood, Robert Woods, Marv Woodson, Barry Word, Danny Wuerffel, Doug Wyatt, Renaldo Wynn

Y

Garo Yepremian, Bob Young, Brian Young, Kevin Young, Tyrone Young, Usama Young, George Youngblood, Dave Yovanovits

Z

Emanuel Zanders, Ray Zellars

List of New Orleans Saints head coaches

The New Orleans Saints are a professional American football team based in New Orleans, Louisiana. They are a member of the South Division of the National Football Conference (NFC) in the National Football League (NFL). The NFL awarded the city of New Orleans the 16th franchise in the league in December 1966, six months after the 89th United States Congress approved the merger of the NFL with the American Football League (AFL) in June of that year. In January 1967, the team was given the current "New Orleans Saints" name, and began playing in their first season in September of that year. Since the franchise's creation, it has been based in New Orleans. The team's home games were originally played at Tulane Stadium from 1967 to 1974 until its demolition, resulting in the relocation of home games to its current stadium as of the 2008 season, the Louisiana Superdome.

The New Orleans Saints have had 14 head coaches in their franchise history. Sean Payton has been the head coach of the Saints since 2006, and the most successful in franchise history. Payton served as the assistant head coach/passing game coordinator and assistant head coach/quarterbacks for the Dallas Cowboys for three seasons before he joined the Saints in 2006. In the 2009 season, he led the team to its first NFC Championship Game and title, Super Bowl (XLIV) appearance, and NFL Championship. Tom Fears, the franchise's first head coach serving from 1967 to 1970, was inducted into the Pro Football Hall of Fame in 1970, and is the only coach to be inducted into the Hall of Fame while spending his entire coaching career with the Saints. Hank Stram, who coached the Saints from 1976 to 1977, and Mike Ditka, who coached the Saints from 1997 to 1999, were also inducted into the Hall of Fame in 2003 and 1988, respectively. Jim E. Mora has coached the most games for the Saints, with 167. He also has the highest winning percentage while coaching the Saints, with .557. Ernie Hefferle and Rick Venturi both have a franchise-worst winning percentage of .125. Jim Haslett, Mora, and Payton are the only head coaches to lead the Saints into the playoffs. Ditka, Mora, and Payton have won the AP Coach of the Year Award and the Sporting News NFL Coach of the Year.

Key

#	Number of coaches
GC	Games coached
W	Wins
L	Losses
T	Ties
Win%	Winning percentage
*	Elected to the Pro Football Hall of Fame
†	Spent entire professional head coaching career with Saints
*†	Elected to the Pro Football Hall of Fame and spent entire professional head coaching career with the Saints

Coaches

Note: Statistics are correct through the end of the 2009 NFL Season

#	Name	Term	Regular Season					Playoffs				Achievements	Reference
			GC	W	L	T	Win%	GC	W	L	Win%		
1	Tom Fears*†	–	49	13	34	2	.277	—	—	—	—		
2	J.D. Roberts†	–	35	7	25	3	.219	—	—	—	—		
3	John North†	–	34	11	23	0	.324	—	—	—	—		
4	Ernie Hefferle†		8	1	7	0	.125	—	—	—	—		
5	Hank Stram*	–	28	7	21	0	.250	—	—	—	—		
6	Dick Nolan	–	44	15	29	0	.341	—	—	—	—		
7	Dick Stanfel†		4	1	3	0	.250	—	—	—	—		
8	Bum Phillips	–	69	27	42	0	.391	—	—	—	—		

9	Wade Phillips		4	1	3	0	.250	—	—	—	—		
10	Jim E. Mora	–	167	93	74	0	.557	4	0	4	.000	AP NFL Coach of the Year (1987) UPI NFL Coach of the Year (1987)	
11	Rick Venturi		8	1	7	0	.125	—	—	—	—		
12	Mike Ditka*	−1999	48	15	33	0	.313	—	—	—	—		
13	Jim Haslett	–	96	45	51	0	.469	2	1	1	.500	AP NFL Coach of the Year (2000)	
14	Sean Payton†	−present	64	38	26	0	.594	5	4	1	.800	AP NFL Coach of the Year (2006)	

Retired Numbers

Jim Taylor (American football)

James Charles "Jim" Taylor (born September 20, 1935) is a former professional American football fullback in the National Football League. Taylor played for ten seasons, from 1958-67. He is a member of the Pro Football Hall of Fame, inducted in the summer of 1976.

He was a running back for the Green Bay Packers from 1958-66, and for the New Orleans Saints in their first season of 1967.

High school and college career

"Jimmy" Taylor was a star athlete at Baton Rouge High in Baton Rouge, LA. He played college football at LSU and was an All-American in 1957.

Professional career

Green Bay Packers

Taylor was selected by the Packers in the second round of the 1958 NFL Draft, the 15th overall pick. He holds many Packers' records, including career rushing yards, touchdowns, single-season touchdowns. He won the NFL rushing title in 1962, the only season that Jim Brown did not lead the league during his nine year career. Taylor's single-season yardage mark (1474) was not surpassed by a Packer until Ahman Green ran for 1883 yards in 2003 (a 16 game season as opposed to the 14 game 1962 season). At retirement, Taylor's 83 career rushing touchdowns placed him behind only Jim Brown.

Taylor was a member of four Packer NFL championship teams (1961, 1962, 1965, and 1966), where he was teamed in the backfield with halfback Paul Hornung. In the Packers 16-7 championship win over the New York Giants in 1962, Taylor set a championship record with 31 carries (for 85 yards) and scored Green Bay's only touchdown of the game. In Green Bay's 1965 championship win, he rushed for 97 yards. In January 1967, Taylor and the Packers played in Super Bowl I, in which they easily defeated the Kansas City Chiefs. Taylor was the top rusher of the game with 56 rushing yards and a touchdown (with his score being the first rushing touchdown in Super Bowl history).

Although not exceptional in size (6-0, 214 lbs.), Taylor was a physical fullback who often won legendary duels with linebacker Sam Huff. Taylor was selected to five consecutive Pro Bowls from

1960-64. He fumbled only 34 times in the 2,173 times he handled the ball (1.56% of his touches.)

New Orleans Saints

In 1967, Taylor played a season with the expansion New Orleans Saints; a year later Jim Taylor retired from pro football. Jim Taylor will always be remembered as a good and honest man, a man who took care of his business with class and dignity.

He finished his career with 8,597 yards and 83 rushing touchdowns, highlighted by his five straight 1,000-yard rushing seasons from 1960-1964. Taylor also caught 225 passes for 1756 yards and 10 touchdowns, and returned 7 kickoffs for 185 yards, giving him a total of 10,539 net yards and 93 touchdowns. His 8,207 rushing yards with the Packers remained a franchise record until Ahman Green surpassed it on November 8, 2009.

Personal life

Taylor currently is in charge of a company called PDG.

External links

- Pro Football Hall of Fame [1] - Jim Taylor
- Jim Taylor's NFL statistics [2]
- Gallery of Jim Taylor football cards [3]

Doug Atkins

Douglas Leon Atkins (born May 8, 1930 in Humboldt, Tennessee) is a former American football defensive end who played for the Cleveland Browns, Chicago Bears and New Orleans Saints in the National Football League. He played college football at the University of Tennessee under legendary head coach Robert Neyland. He is a member of the College Football Hall of Fame and the Pro Football Hall of Fame.

Atkins was a fierce defender who was known for using his immense size and agility to his advantage. At 6'8", Atkins would often bat passes down at the line of scrimmage and would use his skills as a high jump champion to leapfrog blockers and get to the quarterback. Atkins was one of the first great exclusively defensive players in professional football and, along with fellow Hall of Famer Gino Marchetti, revolutionized the defensive end position.

College career

Atkins originally went to Tennessee on a basketball scholarship, but once football coach General Robert R. Neyland saw his combination of size and agility, he was recruited for the grid team. After he earned All-America honors in 1952, the Cleveland Browns selected him with their first choice in the 1953 NFL Draft. Atkins also played on the 1951 Tennessee Volunteers football team that won the national championship. Atkins is one of the few players in Tennessee history to have his number retired. He was considered one of, if not the, most dominant defensive players in SEC history. Atkins was the only unanimous selection to the SEC All Quarter-Century team and was selected as the overall SEC "Player of the Quarter-Century" for the years 1950-1975.

Professional career

Atkins began his playing career with the Cleveland Browns, but his peak years of his 17-year career came with the Chicago Bears. Atkins' first two seasons were played with the Browns before he was traded to the Bears in 1955. In Chicago, Atkins quickly became the leader of a devastating defensive unit. With the Bears, Atkins was a First Team All-Pro selection in 1958, 1960, 1961, and 1963; along with being a starter in the Pro Bowl in eight of his last nine years with Chicago. Before the 1967 season, Atkins requested a trade from Chicago and was traded to the New Orleans Saints, with whom he would end his career in 1969.

Honors

Atkins is a member of both the College Football Hall of Fame and the Pro Football Hall of Fame. He has also been inducted into the Chicagoland Sports Hall of Fame. His collegiate jersey number, 91, was retired by the University of Tennessee in 2005.

Even though he only played three seasons for New Orleans, the club retired his #81, one of two numbers retired by the franchise. The other, #31, belongs to Hall of Fame fullback Jim Taylor, a long-time rival of Atkins during Taylor's days with the Green Bay Packers.

The NFL Network ranked him as the #9 Pass Rusher of All Time in its Top Ten show.

External links

* *Pro Football Hall of Fame:* Member profile [1]

Sam Mills

Samuel Davis "Sam" Mills, Jr. (June 3, 1959 - April 18, 2005) was an American football linebacker who played twelve seasons in the National Football League for the New Orleans Saints and Carolina Panthers.

Early life

Sam Mills was born in Neptune, New Jersey and attended high school in Long Branch, New Jersey. Mills was a standout football player at Long Branch High School, which honors him to this day by hanging his high school jersey and his NFL jersey in the school gym.

USFL

He attended college at Montclair State University. Told he was too small to play in the NFL, he played with the Philadelphia/Baltimore Stars of the USFL for three years. During that time (wearing #54), he became known in the league for both his tenacity on the field and his leadership off it. His speed, surprising for a man of his size, earned him the nickname "The Field Mouse." When Stars head coach Jim Mora left the team to coach the NFL's New Orleans Saints, Mills followed his mentor.

NFL

New Orleans Saints

During his tenure with the Saints, Mills was an anchor of the defense. He was a member of the vaunted "Dome Patrol," the stellar linebacking corps that led a ferocious Saints defense in the early 1990s. Mills earned four Pro Bowl appearances with the Saints in 1987, 1988, 1991, and 1992.

Carolina Panthers

Mills became a free agent at the end of the 1994 NFL season, and was signed by the expansion Carolina Panthers. Mills became a veteran leader for the young team, the only player to start every game during the Panthers' first three seasons. An interception in a 1995 season game sealed the Panthers first ever victory in franchise history against the New York Jets. His career rebirth gave him a fifth Pro Bowl appearance in 1996 at the age of 37. After retiring in 1997, Mills stayed with the organization as a linebackers coach.

Sam Mills holds the NFL record for the oldest player to return a fumble for a touchdown (37 years, 174 days).

After football

Mills played 12 seasons in the NFL and recorded 1,319 tackles, 20.5 sacks, 11 interceptions and four touchdowns while starting 173 of 181 games. He is the only player in the Carolina Panthers Hall of Honor. There is also a statue of him outside of Bank Of America stadium in Charlotte. Mills was named to the NFL All-Pro team three times in 1991, 1992, and 1996. He was elected to both the Louisiana Sports Hall of Fame (1991) and the Sports Hall of Fame of New Jersey (1993).

Mills was diagnosed with intestinal cancer in August 2003. Though he was told he had only a few months to live, he underwent chemotherapy and radiation and continued to coach. He was an inspirational force in the Panthers' post-season run to Super Bowl XXXVIII. His plea to "Keep Pounding" in an emotional speech before the Panthers' victory over the Dallas Cowboys later became the name of a fund to sponsor cancer research programs. Mills died at his home in Charlotte, North Carolina on the morning of April 18, 2005. He was 45.

Mills' number 51 was retired by the Panthers at the start of the 2005 NFL season. The home field of the Montclair State University Red Hawks was named Sam Mills Stadium in his honor. Mills was inducted into the College Football Hall of Fame in 2009. His son Sam Mills III holds the position of Quality Control - Defense for the Carolina Panthers.

Rickey Jackson

Rickey Anderson Jackson (born March 20, 1958 in Pahokee, Florida) is a former American football linebacker in the NFL for the New Orleans Saints (1981–1993) and the San Francisco 49ers (1994–1995). In 1997, Jackson was inducted into the New Orleans Saints Hall of Fame. Jackson won a Super Bowl ring with the 49ers in Super Bowl XXIX one year before retiring. On February 6, 2010, Rickey Jackson was elected into the Pro Football Hall of Fame.

Early years

Jackson's first name was originally spelled "Ricky": he says he changed it himself in high school. Jackson played football and basketball at Pahokee High School in Florida. He totalled 188 tackles and caught 21 passes for 8 touchdowns as a tight end. In 2007 he was named to the Florida High School Association All-Century Team which selected the Top 33 players in the 100 year history of high school football in the state of Florida's history. His nickname, "City Champ", came from his days at Pahokee; Jackson has variously said that he chose the name himself, or was given it because of his dominating play against other towns.

College career

Jackson was known as "the other end" at the University of Pittsburgh due to the presence of Hugh Green playing the RDE in the Panthers 5-2 defense which ranked #1 nationally in 1980. Although overshadowed by Green, Jackson was a Second-team All-America choice as a senior in 1980 and was also a First-team All-Big East selection. In 1979, as a junior he was a Second-team All-Big East choice and an honorable mention All-America by AP and The Sporting News.

Jackson ended his career with 290 total tackles, 166 of the unassisted. He also finished with 21 sacks, four passes defensed and three interceptions. In 1977 as a freshman he totaled 15 tackles and 2 interceptions, one returned for a touchdown. In 1978 as s sophomore he made 27 tackles (21 solo) and recorded five sacks. In 1979 he had 111 tackles (47 unassisted) and 4 sacks and recovered two fumbles. Against Army, in 1980, Jackson was the Sports Illustrated Player of the Week with a 12 tackle, 3 sacks, forced fumble, interception, and a blocked punt-performance. In 1980 he led the team with 137 tackles (87 solo) had 12 sacks, broke up four passes, recovered 4 fumbles and intercepted a pass. In 1980 he won a second weekly honor when he was chosen the ABC/Chevrolet Player-of-the-Game versus Penn State.

Jackson made 14 tackles in the Pittsburgh Gator Bowl win and he also played in the Senior Bowl, where he was a team captain and he was the MVP of the East-West Shrine Game.

Professional career

Drafted in the second round of the 1981 NFL Draft (53rd overall) from the University of Pittsburgh, Jackson was a member of the first Bum Phillips draft in New Orleans. He played in all 16 games his rookie season and was named to the NFL All-rookie team. In 1983 he was First-team All-NFC, the first of seven seasons in which he'd receive post-season honors in the NFL, including being six-time Pro Bowl selection (1983, 1984, 1985, 1986, 1992, 1993). Jackson was a four-time First-team All-Pro and a two-time Second-team All-Pro selection.

Jackson recorded 10 or more sacks in six different seasons and led the NFL in fumble recoveries in 1990 and 1991. He finished his career with 136 (8 unofficial in 1981) sacks and 8 interceptions, which he returned for 68 yards. He also recovered 29 fumbles. At the time of his retirement, his 28 defensive fumble recoveries were the second most in NFL history behind Jim Marshall's 29. He still leads the Saints in career sacks with the team with 123.

In his entire 13 seasons as a Saint, Jackson missed only 2 games, and those 2 games were a result of an automobile accident he suffered in 1989. He played the remainder of the 1989 season with his jaw wired and wearing a special helmet, still managing to accumulate 7-1/2 sacks on the year.

He was a member of the Saints' famed "Dome Patrol", a four-man linebacking corps which the NFL Network ranked as the best in NFL history. In his first year as a finalist in 2010, Jackson was elected to the Pro Football Hall of Fame. He is the first member of the Hall of Fame to be inducted primarily for his contributions as a Saint.

In the NFL Record Books: Source (at time of his retirement following 1995 season)

• [2nd] Most Opponents Fumbles Recovered, Career – 28

• [3rd] Most Sacks, Career – 128.0

• [Tied for 3rd] Most Opponents Fumbles Recovered, Season – 7 (1990)

Saints records held by Jackson: Source

(Records through the 1993 season, Jackson's final season with New Orleans)

• [1st] Most Games – 195

• [1st] Most Sacks, Career – 123.0 (includes unofficial 8.0 sacks in 1981)

• [Tied for 1st] Most Seasons – 13

• [1st] Most Opponents Fumbles Recovered, Career – 26

• [1st] Most Opponents Fumbles Recovered, Season – 7 (1990)

• [Tied for 1st] Most Sacks, Game – 4 (at Atlanta, Dec. 14, 1986; at Detroit, Sept. 18, 1988)

External links

- Career Stats [1]

Article Sources and Contributors

New Orleans Saints *Source*: http://en.wikipedia.org/?oldid=376598972 *Contributors*: Arxiloxos

History of the New Orleans Saints *Source*: http://en.wikipedia.org/?oldid=374866285 *Contributors*: 1 anonymous edits

List of New Orleans Saints seasons *Source*: http://en.wikipedia.org/?oldid=355550916 *Contributors*: Arxiloxos

Louisiana Superdome *Source*: http://en.wikipedia.org/?oldid=376670207 *Contributors*: Shyguy1991

Effect of Hurricane Katrina on the New Orleans Saints *Source*: http://en.wikipedia.org/?oldid=344124698 *Contributors*: Dale Arnett

2006 New Orleans Saints season *Source*: http://en.wikipedia.org/?oldid=364793240 *Contributors*: 1 anonymous edits

2007 New Orleans Saints season *Source*: http://en.wikipedia.org/?oldid=360274264 *Contributors*:

2008 New Orleans Saints season *Source*: http://en.wikipedia.org/?oldid=357937973 *Contributors*: Bento00

2009 New Orleans Saints season *Source*: http://en.wikipedia.org/?oldid=376445237 *Contributors*: Arxiloxos

2010 New Orleans Saints season *Source*: http://en.wikipedia.org/?oldid=376120974 *Contributors*: Svick

Super Bowl XLIV *Source*: http://en.wikipedia.org/?oldid=375724826 *Contributors*:

Drew Brees *Source*: http://en.wikipedia.org/?oldid=376305834 *Contributors*: Arxiloxos

List of New Orleans Saints players *Source*: http://en.wikipedia.org/?oldid=366911216 *Contributors*: Jwalte04

List of New Orleans Saints head coaches *Source*: http://en.wikipedia.org/?oldid=343031955 *Contributors*: 1 anonymous edits

Jim Taylor (American football) *Source*: http://en.wikipedia.org/?oldid=375466311 *Contributors*: 1 anonymous edits

Doug Atkins *Source*: http://en.wikipedia.org/?oldid=361210476 *Contributors*: 1 anonymous edits

Sam Mills *Source*: http://en.wikipedia.org/?oldid=367571789 *Contributors*:

Rickey Jackson *Source*: http://en.wikipedia.org/?oldid=376703351 *Contributors*: Arxiloxos

LaVergne, TN USA
19 December 2010
209378LV00003B/98/P

[8]